Promises
to
Keep

the Calling,
Character,
and Cost
of Commitment

I Peter
2:91=

Prentice A. Meador

PROMISES TO KEEP

Published by 21st Century Christian Publishing, Nashville, Tennessee.

Table of Contents

1	Semper Fidelis	11
2	It Was His Passion	29
3	Out of the Masses	49
4	Why Is Whole Religion So Hard To Sell?	71
5	The Death of Trust	93
6	If It's Broken, Fix It	119
7	A Cross, A Yoke, A Towel	139
8	Jesus Never Ran	157
9	For Better, For Worse	179
10	Saving Your Child's Life	209
11	Honor Your Father and Mother	223
12	Throwing Away Our Scorecards	239
13	The Guns Are Silent	259

Dedicated to

Scott and Lori Ann
Mark and Shelli
Doug and Kimberly

You make life lots of fun.

Acknowledgments

There are lots of people who have urged, cajoled, encouraged, and brow-beaten me to get this book done.

Special thanks to . . .

Barry Brewer, my publisher. Thanks for suggesting this book and that I do it. You stayed on my back, and I will always be grateful. You taught me something about commitment as you have endured through cancer.

Mary Hollingsworth and Linda Varnado, my editors. You both knew what my book needed and had the courage to tell me. Thanks for reading the entire manuscript, asking questions, and making valuable suggestions. You're tough!

Cathy Brown, my editorial assistant. You're not only a neat member of our family, but a very able consultant. You helped me focus the text, and it was just plain fun working with you.

Malinda Gowan, my secretary. You do more than answer my phone, organize my life, and type my stuff. You're the best. Thank you so much for typing the entire deal.

Bob Chisholm, my good friend. Thanks for valuable suggestions. You have an unbelievable talent as a wordsmith.

Dave Malone, my associate. Thanks for making helpful suggestions on several chapters. As "brave Dave," you did it again.

Barbara Meador, my dear wife. What can I say? Thanks for giving the title to this book. You're always there for me. You make commitment more than a word. My deepest love and respect to you.

To members of my family. Thanks for living as committed people. You gave me lots of fodder for this book.

I bear complete responsibility for the weaknesses in this book. They would have been far greater without the outstanding support of those mentioned above.

God, my Father. He has taught me most about the real meaning of promises. What would life be without Him?

Prentice A. Meador, Jr.

Foreword

I've never seen a book that did such a great job of tying together the Bible and what we must do in our everyday living. Prentice makes it evident that we need to do both—what God wants us to do first and what we must do for our fellowman as well. My wish is that everyone could read this book and take it to heart.

I've known Prentice as a preacher and a personal friend for over thirty years. His preaching and teaching have always been sound and committed to the truth and the spreading of the gospel. The results of his commitment are easy to see, both in the tremendous growth of the Prestoncrest congregation and in his personal life, including his many close friends and the thousands of people he has influenced all through his ministry.

Has there ever been a time in the history of our country when commitment is needed more? This volume, with its many wonderful examples from our everyday lives alongside personal histories from the Old and New Testaments, shows us exactly what commitment means and how such dedication makes us better and truly happier people.

Byron Nelson
Roanoke, Texas

Introduction

Commitment today is as fickle as the promises of the petals of a daisy, alternating between "he loves me," and "he loves me not." What will the last petal say?

We have evolved into a society of on-again, off-again people, vacillating between ardor and apathy. One day we're hot; the next day we're not. We make lifelong vows but break them in a moment—vows to God, to husbands and wives, to children, to friends, to business partners and associates, and even to ourselves. Our word, which once was our solemn and trusted bond, is now often broken and unreliable.

Is it any wonder that church budgets go unmet, that young men and women are wary of getting married, that teenagers don't respect their parents or teachers, that lawyers are busy drafting no-loophole contracts between business partners, and friends are leery of loaning each other money? Should we be surprised that, without true commitment, Christians are indistinguishable from the world, that the mission of the church goes unaccomplished, and that even Christian homes are disintegrating in record numbers?

Even God himself must see our wavering devotion to him as a they-love-me, they-love-me-not spiritual romance. We're spastically unfaithful, which must feel to him like an insult—a slap in the face from the very ones he loves so dearly and gave so much to save.

When did real commitment die? And how can we resurrect it in all the different areas of life? What must we do to restore trust to its pedestal and put commitment back into our daily lives?

Whatever it takes, however difficult it is, we must begin to do it. We must begin today!

Prentice A. Meador, Jr.
Dallas, Texas

Do as you promised, so that your name will be great forever.

2 Samuel 7:25, NIV

Chapter 1
Semper Fidelis

My high school history teacher made history come alive. He didn't just lecture, he conveyed his love for American history with passion. When we came to the story of the Battle of Okinawa in the South Pacific during World War II, he suddenly began to cry. He actually stopped his lecture and cried openly. As sixteen-year-old high school students, we had no idea what he was feeling.

Finally, he said in a broken voice, "I will have to tell you why I'm crying. As my brother came off his landing vessel in Okinawa, a Japanese machine gun cut him in half. He was killed in the battle that I'm telling you about."

Now my teacher was not just a history teacher—he was a brother. As he talked to us, he could see his own brother dead on the beach—dreams dashed, hopes broken, potential wasted, life snuffed out. There would be no more family Christmas celebrations or Thanksgiving turkey dinners. No more worship services or family football games. I was listening to something that I didn't understand and seeing things I didn't quite grasp. What causes a young Marine to give his life—all of it, completely, totally, without question?

Always Faithful

Isn't it interesting how certain phrases stick in your mind? Public relations firms design ads on television and radio with catch words that bring to mind their products. Every year ADDY Awards are presented for some of the most memorable catch words and their ads. For example, when you hear the phrase "Like a rock," you probably think of Chevrolet. "The best a man can get" brings to mind Gillette. And everyone knows that "The Real Thing" is Coca Cola. You watch or hear these commercials a few times, and the words stay frozen in your mind.

Here is a phrase that may not be quite so familiar. It's found at the United States Marine Memorial in Washington, D.C. As you approach the Memorial, you see the stars and stripes being raised on the Iwo Jima Memorial where the U.S. Marines defeated the Japanese in January 1945. As your eyes move from Old Glory down the statue, you see two Latin words at the base of the memorial: *Semper Fidelis*—always faithful. These words describe the costliest battle in the South Pacific: Iwo Jima.

On an early morning in February 1945, U.S. Marine divisions launched an attack on the beaches of Iwo Jima. It would have been difficult for anyone in command to have predicted the cost of the battle that was about to take place. After all, the eight-square-mile island was only five miles long. In 1887 Japan annexed Iwo Jima, along with two smaller islands, to form the Volcano Islands chain. Since the island was only seven hundred fifty miles south of Tokyo, Iwo Jima served as a stepping-stone for the Americans in 1945. Before the battle of Iwo Jima, Japanese fighter planes attacked American bombers from bases on the island. In a raging hand-to-hand battle, over six thousand men, including more than fifty-eight hundred men of the Third, Fourth and Fifth U.S. Marine Divisions, gave their lives to capture Iwo Jima. At the southern end of the island stood the 546-foot-high Mt. Suribachi, a volcano. A handful of valiant Marines raised the flag of the United States on top of the mountain. Perhaps no

symbol in all of American history has come to symbolize better the meaning of *semper fidelis* —always faithful.

Semper fidelis—a commitment that is made by all
enlisting United States Marines, guys like my history
teacher's brother. Always faithful on land, in the air,
and on the seas. Whenever danger lurks, whether convenient or inconvenient, whether married or single,
whether in pain or in health—always faithful.

Our teacher's brother got up that morning somewhere in the South Pacific and must have thought, *I'm
willing to die for the freedoms of the United States of
America. I'm willing to lay it on the line. I'm willing to
take that Island, even if it takes my life* . . . and it did.
That's called commitment, the keeping of promises he
made when he enlisted in the Marines.

Commitment

Commitment blends together all that we as
Christians hold dear, without any pretense or embarrassment. Our faith and convictions are to be lived out
fully and completely in life. Commitment inspires us to
remember who we are and where we are going. It cov-
ers the most important relationships we know in life,
such as marriage and parenting, relationships with
God and the church of Jesus Christ, and in the work-

place. Commitment is not about the edge of the target; it's about dead center, the bull's eye.

When I was a boy, my dad said this to me: "Anything worth doing is worth doing right!" Several coaches in my sports career said something similar to me: "Give it 110 percent!" Commitment puts steel in our nerves in times of turmoil and change, and it reminds us of the great heritage we have.

Commitment carries us back to promises and vows that God made to people like Abraham, Isaac, and Jacob and causes us to remember that the Son of God made promises to us, too. In Christian tones, commitment speaks of forgotten stories of strong people like Esther, Job, David, Peter, Lydia, and Paul.

Voices cry out to us daily. On Monday morning we hear the voice that says, "Look out for number one." All week long we hear a voice say, "Do whatever feels good." By Friday another voice says, "It's *your* weekend; have fun; do what *you* want to do."

Yet Christians hear an overriding Voice from heaven saying, "You are my beloved child. You have committed yourself to me. Honor that commitment, and honor all commitments that you make in your relationships." How do we learn to listen intently to that Voice above all others?

Commitment argues with a world of fine print and broken promises. It quarrels with skyrocketing divorce rates, abused children, and political demagoguery. Whatever happened to commitment?

What Is Commitment?

What does it mean to be *always faithful*? Commitment isn't easy, admittedly, but it is the glue of relationships. It is the stuff of genuineness and real, authentic attachments. You can't have a good marriage without commitment. You can't lovingly care for your elderly parents without it. You can't rear children well unless you are committed to them. To follow Christ and remain in His church throughout your entire life, you must be totally committed to Him. Commitment is what holds us together.

Commitment speaks a vocabulary of forgotten words like courage, loyalty, duty, honor, discipline, perseverance, integrity, sacrifice, passion, intensity, fervor —words that stick like glue. These are words you don't hear much anymore. In our fast-changing world they are a forgotten vocabulary.

To grasp an understanding of commitment, let's explore the links in the chain of commitment through three great stories in the Word of God. As Elie Wiesel reminds us, "God created man because he loves stories."

A Story of Loyalty

I know what loyalty looks like, because I see it in the face of a young Jewish girl whose Persian name is Esther. There is no hype to this life-or-death story. The intolerant, offensive Xerxes I ruled Persia in 483 B.C. from his royal palace in Susa. At the suggestion of his advisor Haman, Xerxes issued a decree to exterminate all of the Jews living in Persia because their customs were different. Esther was close to the king—so close that she was the only hope for saving her nation. So her Uncle Mordecai said to her, "Don't think because you are in the king's house that you alone of all the Jews will escape" (Esther 4:13).

Fear struck her face, because no one looks death in the eye without fear. Yet she responded, "If I perish, I perish" (Esther 4:16). Esther risked her very life to go before the king. Calmly and carefully, Esther made a case for the Jewish people: "If I have favor with you, O king, and if it pleases your majesty, grant me my life—this is my petition. And spare my people—this is my request. For I and my people have been sold for destruction and slaughter and annihilation. If we had merely been sold as male and female slaves, I would have kept quiet, because no such distress would justify disturbing the king."

Xerxes angrily retorted, "Where is the man who has dared to do such a thing?" Esther said, "The adversary and enemy is Haman." In a rage, Xerxes ordered the hanging of Haman, and the Jewish nation was saved by Queen Esther.

What is the link in the chain of commitment that is so evident in the attitude of Esther? Isn't it loyalty—loyalty at all costs? *"If I perish, I perish."* No excuses. No situation ethics. No backing down. She was playing hardball and showing loyalty to the core. *Always faithful.*

A Story of Integrity

I have seen integrity, too. I have seen it in Daniel's consistency between his talk and his walk. I have heard it in his daily prayers which were forbidden by the government. He was not just a man of appearances. He backed up his talk by overcoming overwhelming obstacles.

Nebuchadnezzar, king of Babylon, singled out several young Jewish men for palace service, but Daniel and the other young men refused the lifestyle of the royal palace. They entered into the king's private service after three years of special training and excelled in wisdom and understanding. Inflamed by jealousy, the administrators of the king's government set a trap for Daniel. They seduced the king into declaring that anyone who prayed to another god other than the golden image erected by the Babylonian government would be thrown into the lions' den.

"Now when Daniel learned that the decree had been published, he went home to his upstairs room where the windows opened toward Jerusalem. Three times a day he got down on his knees and prayed, giving thanks to his God, just as he had done before" (Daniel 6:10). Why does Daniel continue to pray in the face of death? "At this the administrators and the satraps tried to find grounds for charges against Daniel in his conduct of government affairs, but they were unable to do so. They could find no corruption in him, because he was trustworthy and neither corrupt nor negligent" (Daniel 6:4).

Here was the face of integrity. Threatened with death by lions he still went straight to his window the moment he read the newly published instruction not to pray to God, and what did he do? He prayed to God. *Always faithful.* He opened his windows, got down on his knees, and prayed three times a day just as he had done before. Integrity—it is one of the most powerful links in commitment's chain.

A Story of Sacrifice

I have also seen the clear, firm, and strong face of sacrifice. At some point, Stephen felt the grace and mercy of Christ. He followed Christ and accepted Him as Lord and Savior, developing a deep conviction of faith. His was not a faith turned on and off like a faucet but a faith ready to be tested. He had an appointment with pain and suffering when hostile, angry, murderous men surrounded him (Acts 7).

Stephen had to choose between life and death, between renunciation and conviction, between walking away a free man with no loyalty or being stoned to death for his convictions. Sizing up all of the risks, he chose to state powerfully his convictions in behalf of Jesus Christ by remaining *always faithful*. "While they were stoning him, Stephen prayed, 'Lord Jesus, receive my spirit.' Then he fell on his knees and cried out, 'Lord, do not hold this sin against them.' When he had said this, he fell asleep" (Acts 7:59, 60).

Here is the third link in the chain of commitment: willingness to sacrifice yourself—to lay it on the line every day. "I die daily," claims a committed Paul; and commitment says, "Given all of the risks, I'm willing to give my life."

How Do We Know If We're Always Faithful?

That's the practical question, isn't it? Fortunately, the Bible gives us answers. Commitment is being single-minded, wholehearted, focused. "No one can serve two masters. Either he will hate the one and love the other, or he will be devoted to the one and despise the other. You cannot serve both God and Money" (Matthew 6:24). The classic example of spiritual schizophrenia is Judas Iscariot. With one hand he tried to hold on to the Savior, and with the other hand he tried to hold on to the thirty pieces of silver. His dualism split him in two and led to his suicide. You *can't* serve two masters. It's impossible. No way! Forget it. Give it up, because it *ain't* gonna happen. *And* there are no exceptions to the rule. You will surely, without fail, hate one and love the other.

C. S. Lewis, in *Mere Christianity,* said this single-mindedness changes you completely. "Christ says, 'Give me All. I don't want so much of your time, and so much of your money, and so much of your work; I want You. I have not come to torment your natural self, but to kill it. No half-measures are any good. I don't want to cut off a branch here and a branch there, I want to have the whole tree down. Hand over the whole natural self, all the desires which you think innocent as well as the ones which you think wicked—the whole outfit. I will give you a new self, instead. In fact, I will give you Myself: My own will shall become yours.'"

We call it conversion or transformation. When we become committed, we become focused upon God and Christ. That focus gives us wholeheartedness, single-mindedness, a devotion to Christ. Because of what He has done for us, we give ourselves to Him.

We also know that we are *always faithful* when our attitudes become "all, or nothing at all." Esther, Daniel, and Stephen—their attitude was "all, or nothing at all." David, the man after God's own heart, said, "Seek the Lord with your whole heart." I strongly believe in doing things totally. Don't do it part way, but do it 110 percent. If you are playing ball, play the best you can play, or don't wear the uniform. If you plan to be in business, study as hard as you possibly can, and become the best you can be. If you are going to be a parent, be the best father or mother you can be. Don't just do it half way. As David Lloyd George, one of my favorite British Prime Ministers, said, "The most dangerous thing in the world is to attempt to leap a chasm in two jumps."

Jesus knew something of that "all, or nothing at all" spirit: "Anyone who loves his father or mother more than me is not worthy of me; anyone who loves his son or daughter more than me is not worthy of me; and anyone who does not take his cross and follow me is not worthy of me. Whoever finds his life will lose it, and whoever loses his life for my sake will find it" (Matthew 10:37, 38).

It's all, or nothing at all when we follow Jesus. He will not be number two or three on our priority lists. He will be first, or He won't be on the lists at all. Jesus calls us to an exclusive relationship with Him, not to sinlessness but to single-mindedness. We are His bride, and He is our groom—no bigamy is allowed. I am reminded of the classic hymn "True-Hearted, Whole-hearted" by Frances Havergal and George Stebbins:

> True-hearted, whole-hearted, faithful and loyal,
> King of our lives, by Thy grace we will be.
> Under the standard exalted and royal,
> Strong in Thy strength we will battle for Thee.
>
> True-hearted, whole-hearted, Savior all-glorious!
> Take Thy great power and reign there alone,
> Over our wills and affections victorious,
> Freely surrendered and wholly Thine own.

How do we know if we are promise keepers, committed, *always faithful?* We never quit! Jesus says to the church at Smyrna, "Be faithful even to the point of death, and I will give you the crown of life" (Revelation 2:10). Regardless of the trials, tribulations, accusations, what people think of us, and the way we are treated, we never, never, never quit. We decide, way down deep in our willpower, that we will follow our Lord all the way to death.

It has been my experience over the years in ministering to people who are dying, that they die the same way they lived. It has been my privilege to be at the bedsides of many Christians who, during their lives decided to follow Jesus Christ, and right up through the death experience were saying, "The Lord is my shepherd, I shall not want" (Psalm 23:1). They were always faithful, even to the point of death.

―――――――――――――――
―――――――――――――――

As she rested in her bed in Baylor Hospital in Dallas, Diane Songer began to face her last hours as a leukemia patient. Her doctors had used every available medical technique, including a bone marrow transplant, to treat her. As I stood beside her bed, I noticed how tired and fatigued she was and what a struggle it was for her to speak.

I first knew Diane as a searcher, a seeker, a person looking for God and a deeper relationship with Christ. She had given me the opportunity to be a part of her spiritual life. Her Christian commitment had already reached out and touched the lives of family and friends. She looked up through weak eyes and made me promise again that I would conduct her service just as she had outlined in her letter to me. Later, I opened her letter and read her handwritten directions:

> *I don't want a lot of statistics about ME. The only statistic that matters is that I loved the Lord my God with all my heart and served him imperfectly, but in complete and total forgiveness, that I loved this world and those in it, and that I lived happy, joyous and FREE!*

Diane never quit, not even in death. In his book *The Company of the Committed,* Elton Trueblood draws this picture of a committed Christian:

> A Christian is a person who confesses that, amidst the manifold and confusing voices heard in the world, there is one Voice which supremely wins his full

assent, uniting all his powers, intellectual and emotional, into a single pattern of self-giving. That Voice is Jesus Christ. A Christian not only believes that He was; he believes in Him with all his heart and strength and mind. Christ appears to the Christian as the one stable point or fulcrum in all the relativities of history. Once the Christian has made this primary commitment he still has perplexities, but he begins to know the joy of being used for a mighty purpose, by which his little life is dignified.

Becoming committed to Christ is an inside job. Sometimes we look to the outside, but this is a matter of our heart, and it cannot be over emphasized. Take a good look inside yourself; then commit yourself to Christ. It's your first and primary commitment. As Herbert Butterfield put it, "Follow Christ, and for the rest remain uncommitted." In other words, *semper fidelis!*

Thinking It Through

Opening Your Heart

"Commitment isn't easy, admittedly, but it is the glue of relationships."

- What words come to your mind when you think of "commitment"?
- Describe or profile a committed person that you have known.

Digging Into God's Word

Turn to Hebrews 11 and select one story of commitment from this chapter on faith.

- Why did you select this particular person?
- How does this Old Testament person demonstrate commitment?
- Why does God ask for "faithfulness" when He could ask for so many other things?

Taking It Home

"Being committed to Christ is an inside job."

- When you look inside, what do you see?
- Describe a time when you were tempted to quit, but you didn't.
- Name three things you will do this week to strengthen your personal faith.

Chapter 2
"It Was His Passion"

"MARCH MADNESS"—championship basketball with teams like UCLA, Kentucky, Kansas, North Carolina and Duke, and great players like Pete Maravich, one of basketball's greatest magicians, come to mind. The name Maravich is synonymous with college basketball greatness. While a freshman at Louisiana State University (LSU), he was so exciting to watch that fans would go home after the freshman game because the varsity was not as fun to watch. At LSU, Pete Maravich set forty-three National Collegiate Athletic Association (NCAA) records. He was the first player from college basketball to sign with the National Basketball Association (NBA) for more than a million dollars, and he entered the Hall of Fame the first year he was eligible.

But Pete had begun to drink too much and had become very lonely. It was at this point that he changed his entire life. He searched for something more than fame, money, and pleasure . . . and found it. Pete Maravich decided to change the direction of his life.

James Dobson later wrote this about Maravich: "For the past five years of Maravich's life he couldn't talk five minutes without telling you what Jesus had done in his life. It was his passion." Dobson should know, because he had invited Maravich to be his guest on the *Focus on the Family* radio program. Before the program, Maravich joined Dobson and a few friends for a morning pick-up basketball game. He still loved the game. During a break Maravich said, "I'm not really playing too well today, but I've got to get back into basketball. I feel just great."

Those were the last words Pete Maravich ever spoke. He fell to the floor and died from a heart attack. Dobson and the others administered CPR but could not bring him back. Dobson said that he looked down at the T-shirt Maravich was wearing which said, "Looking unto Jesus." Fame, money, and pleasure meant very little to Maravich at this point in his life; Jesus was what really mattered.

We live in a time when people don't seem to care about many things. As Steve Farrar, in his book *Point Man,* says, "We live in an era when commitment is cheap. It's cheap in marriage, business, politics, and even athletics." Maybe Farrar is wrong; but maybe he's not.

Free Agency Commitment

I'm an old St. Louis Cardinals fan. Names like Enos Slaughter, Stan Musial, and Marty Marion have meant so much to me. I followed their careers year after year, knew their batting averages, and never dreamed the day would come when they wouldn't be with the St. Louis Cardinals team. I've also known some people who worked their entire careers for companies like Genesco, General Electric, Texaco, or Ford. But today we live in a "free agency" world. It's a term that was first used in professional sports to mean that, at a particular point in your contract, you can cut your ties with your team. You no longer legally belong to them, but you become a free agent—on your own, at liberty to "do your own thing." For example, a well known professional baseball player said that he liked the city where he played for a number of years, and he liked the team, but unless he got more money, he would be moving on. You can't blame him, can you? He was only making two million dollars a year.

The "free agency" mindset—performing when it's convenient or when it makes you happy—has spilled over into other areas of life. It takes its toll on marriage, parenting, and the marketplace every day, and it is certainly a major concern in our personal spiritual lives.

C.S. Lewis, in his *Screwtape Letters,* put words in Satan's mouth as Satan advised his nephew, Wormwood, on the strategy of tempting a brand new Christian into sin. Satan said, "It is the Devil's aim not that good men should do evil but that good men should do nothing at all. I, the Devil, will always see to it that there are bad men. Your job, my dear Wormwood, is to provide me with men who do not care."

You can "do religion" as long as it is satisfying or personally convenient, fills your needs, or makes you happy. However, this kind of free agency commitment contrasts boldly with the total commitment Jesus Christ calls for in the New Testament.

Christianity is a Personal Commitment

Christianity begins with Jesus calling us to make *personal* commitments to Him. My wife, Barbara, tells me how *personal* Christianity is, and she's right! Christianity is not a private religion; it is meant to be shared with others. We are called to be the light of the world and the salt of the earth—to do good to all people. Although it's not a *private* religion, it is a very *personal* religion.

Beginning his ministry in Galilee, Jesus walked by the tax collecting area. "As Jesus went on from there, he saw a man named Matthew sitting at the tax collector's booth. 'Follow me,' he told him, and Matthew got up and followed him" (Matthew 9:9-13). There was no crowd, no group, no synagogue, no mass media but instead a one-on-one encounter. Jesus looked right into the face of Matthew and said, "Follow me." It's doubtful that Matthew understood all that those words meant, but Jesus seems to take us where He finds us.

Jesus also walked by the Sea of Galilee where ". . . he saw Simon and his brother Andrew casting a net into the lake, for they were fishermen. 'Come, follow me,' Jesus said, 'and I will make you fishers of men.' At once they left their nets and followed him" (Mark 1:16). Did these fishermen understand the full implications of following Jesus? Did they really think He was the Savior and Lord? Does Jesus require total comprehension, full understanding of the journey before He calls us to follow? Instead, isn't Jesus saying, "I want you to begin to follow me. I'll take you right where you are, with all of your guilt, with all of your problems, with your fishy smelling clothes, with all of your misunderstanding of who I am. I may not be who you think I am, but I am calling you to follow me"—a direct invitation to Peter and Andrew, no one else.

He still calls us, and it is still a personal, one-on-one encounter with the Galilean. Sometimes in large audiences we think that He is calling the masses. Hopefully, as you read the Word of God, even though it may be as a preacher speaks publicly, it becomes a personal call from Jesus for you to follow Him—a direct encounter. Perhaps, you are in a small group and you begin to hear the Word of God speaking to you personally. You are hearing, "Come follow me." You may be surrounded by thousands of people, with problems way over your head, and turned off by religion that seems cold and institutionalized. Yet the call of Jesus Christ is a very personal call. The invitation has your name on it, because Christ is not calling someone else; He's calling you. No one can respond for you, because it's a do-it-yourself religion with a personal call that you alone can answer.

In the Book of Acts, ten different individuals ask, "What must I do to be saved?" Jesus says through Peter, Paul, Philip, or some other teacher, "Follow me." He calls an African nobleman, an Ethiopian who is going home. God interrupts his trip by sending Philip to teach him about Jesus. The text says that Philip began with the very passage that the African man was reading and taught him about the personal call of Jesus Christ. No wonder he confessed Jesus as Lord and was baptized by Philip.

We discover the same story over and over in Acts: Jesus Christ calls different people to become His followers, and with each one He desires a personal relationship. So the African left the desert with more than a religious discussion. He left with a personal relationship with Jesus Christ, because he accepted His invitation. Life for the Ethiopian would never be the same again; it became new, different, and exciting.

Some time after the Bible was written, Augustine wrote this in his *Confessions* regarding the commitment he had made:

> When I was trying to reach a decision about serving the Lord my God, as I had long intended to do, it was I who willed to take this course and again it was I who

willed not to take it. It was I and I alone. But I neither willed to do it nor refused to do it with my full will. So I was at odds with myself. I was throwing myself into confusion. All this happened to me although I did not want it, but it did prove that there was some second mind in me besides my own. . . . When we try to make a decision, we have one soul which is torn between two conflicting wills. Some say that there are two opposing minds within us, one good and the other bad, and that they are in conflict because they spring from two opposing substances or principles.

I understand something of what Augustine was writing, because I recall the struggle of wanting to become a Christian. I wanted it long before I fully committed to it. I remember something about it that caused me not to make the commitment, and I decided to put it off for a while.

A sketch of procrastination appears in Acts when Paul spoke to King Agrippa. When Paul finished presenting Jesus to him, the King was so torn that he said, "Paul, almost you persuade me to become a Christian."

But he was not persuaded. King Agrippa could have really identified with what Augustine later wrote. God voted for Agrippa, but Agrippa didn't vote for God.

It takes a personal commitment of will that finally causes us to establish a personal relationship with Jesus. When you make that personal commitment, it means you will keep your promise to follow Him, regardless of what happens. When you confess that Jesus is the Christ, the Son of God, and make that commitment to follow Him, it is for life. We make few life commitments, but when we decide to follow Jesus, we make a personal, unconditional life commitment of will and heart.

Take Up Your Cross Daily

Jesus doesn't want us just to assent to His existence; He wants us to commit our hearts, lives, souls, and minds to Him by making a personal, lifelong commitment—a promise we plan to keep.

Jesus also calls us to "die daily." This is a disturbing passage: "If anyone would come after me, he must deny himself and take up his cross daily and follow me. For whoever wants to save his life will lose it, but whoever loses his life for me will save it" (Luke 9:23, 24). The passage is disturbing because of the symbol Jesus uses: He says if we follow Him, we must take up the cross daily. I would have preferred for Him to tell us to take up our picnic baskets—to go and enjoy life. But a cross has only one purpose—death—and that is what Jesus is demanding.

How easy it is for me to misunderstand my cross. What is your cross? You might respond that if I knew your husband or wife, I'd know your cross, but it's not your wife, or your husband, or your Aunt Minnie. Look at the words again, "If anyone would come after me, he must deny *himself* and take up his cross daily and follow me." What part of your will must you deny on a daily basis to follow Jesus? To what part of your life must you say no? Materialism? Greed? Pride? Racism? Is there one sin that tempts you easily? What one thing is the most difficult to give up?

A cross intersects the vertical with the horizontal. In a similar way, if you think of the horizontal as your will and the vertical as God's will for you, the point where those two wills intersect is your personal cross. We are all different, having distinct problems. So, your cross may be different from another's. That's the point: For anyone to follow Jesus, he must deny *himself.*

Charles Swindoll says that the trouble with Christianity is that it is so *daily.* Jesus says that the depth of our commitment is measured by our willingness to surrender to the Lord our wills, our sins, and the things we most need to deny . . . daily.

Total Commitment

If this sounds like total commitment, it is. At least twice Paul described his own commitment. While speaking to a group of elders, he said this: "And now, compelled by the Spirit, I am going to Jerusalem, not knowing what will happen to me there. I only know that in every city the Holy Spirit warns me that prison and hardships are facing me. However I consider my life worth nothing to me, if only I may finish the race and complete the task the Lord Jesus has given me—the task of testifying to the gospel of God's grace" (Acts 20:22-24). That's commitment. He started his race, and he needed to finish it. The commitment he had made called him to deny himself every day. Then Paul continued his own story of total commitment:

> After we had been there a number of days,
> a prophet named Agabus came down from
> Judea. Coming over to us, he took Paul's
> belt, tied his own hands and feet with it
> and said, "The Holy Spirit says, 'In this
> way the Jews of Jerusalem will bind the
> owner of this belt and will hand him over

to the Gentiles.'" When we heard this, we
and the people there pleaded with Paul
not to go up to Jerusalem. Then Paul
answered, "Why are you weeping and
breaking my heart? I am ready not only to
be bound, but also to die in Jerusalem for
the name of the Lord Jesus." When he
would not be dissuaded, we gave up and
said, "The Lord's will be done." (Acts
21:10-14)

Paul realized that God voted for him. Now he voted
daily for God.

Jesus calls us to love Him more than we love ourselves. He wants us every day to say "yes" to His
Lordship in our lives. A number of years ago when we
were living in California, the Maurice Hall family was
living in Saigon, Vietnam. It was in the early years of
the involvement of America in Vietnam, and Maurice
dedicated himself to sharing Christ there. One day he
saw some Buddhist priests pour gasoline on themselves, set themselves on fire, and burn to death in the
street. "If these priests are willing to die for a dead
Buddha, I ought to be willing to die for a living Christ,"
Maurice later remarked. It became his life's passion.

Finish the Race

Did you ever run track in school? I remember running in a high school track meet at Vanderbilt. I had finished running the 400-meter race, and I asked one of the guys on the track team who ran the 220, "How did you do?"

He said, "Well, I ran well for 215."

Think about that for a moment. Have you ever been in a 220 race, and you ran only 215? That's all you had in you, so you didn't finish. Have you ever been running a 10K race, but you ran only 9K?

Paul likened commitment to running a race. He said toward the end of his life, "I have finished the race." It was 440 meters, and I ran 440 meters. It was a 10K, and I ran 10K. You and I are not called to run just part of the race and stop. If you have a passion for Jesus Christ, finish the race! Be faithful until death! Keep your promise.

In 490 B.C. the Persians landed on Greek territory. When the Greeks finally won the battle against the Persians, the Greeks sent Phidippides twenty-six miles from Marathon to Athens to deliver the news of their great victory. The instant he had shouted the news, Phidippides dropped dead. He was the first marathon runner, and today marathon races around the globe commemorate his faithfulness and commitment to finish the race in spite of the distance.

The free agency mentality from contemporary athletics has, unfortunately, seeped over into business and into Christian thinking. Some of us decide to start the race, but something happens and we quit. We break under the weight of stress or busy schedules. Once we said, "I believe Jesus is the Christ, the Son of God." We start the race with good intentions, but something happens, perhaps a temptation, a problem, a discouragement, a hurdle of some sort. We run part of the race, and Satan tempts us to quit. Meanwhile Jesus runs ahead of us and motions for us to finish the race.

We are not the first runners to struggle with finishing. An impressive list of runners is found in Hebrews 11—Abraham, Isaac, Jacob, Joseph, Moses, Rahab, Samson, Jephthah, Samuel, and the prophets: "Therefore, since we are surrounded by such a great cloud of witnesses, let us throw off everything that hinders and the sin that so easily entangles, and let us run with perseverance the race marked out for us. Let us fix our eyes on Jesus, the author and perfecter of our faith, who for the joy set before him endured the cross, scorning its shame, and sat down at the right hand of the throne of God" (Hebrews 12:1, 2).

We are in a race, and we are being encouraged. Jesus has already run His race, and He's waiting for us at the finish line. He calls us to focus on the finish line, not to look back but forward to the finish. We must keep our eyes on the goal. And just like Olympic runners who were encircled by a great coliseum of people in the Roman theaters, so you are encircled by a great crowd of spiritual witnesses. People who have lived before you—who have already run their races—are cheering you on. Can you imagine what a thrill it would be, and what stamina it would add to your willpower, if you could see Abraham, Noah, Paul, and Peter clapping their hands and hear them shouting, "Come on, you can make it! Keep running! Don't quit!"

I was finishing the Turkey Trot (a Thanksgiving day race) in Dallas and approaching the 7.5 mile marker with just a half-mile left. But fatigue and discouragement began to slow me down. I needed to make one final turn, and the finish line would almost be in sight, but I didn't know if I could hold out or not. Just as I made the turn, a runner who had already finished the race must have recognized my struggle. I'll never forget his words of encouragement: "You can make it. The end is near." I did. In competition you learn that you're not so much running against other runners as you are running against yourself to finish a race, and you discover that it is more important to finish than to win.

Our daughter, Kimberly, ran in her first marathon at Ohio State University. The temperature was a frigid 21 degrees. The wind-chill factor was -4 degrees. Over seven thousand runners started the race. Hundreds dropped out by the end of the first five miles. Here's how Kimberly described it:

> The cold starts with your extremities and works its way up your legs and arms. My legs were just frozen. At twenty-four miles, I started hitting my legs and couldn't feel them. Over a thousand runners dropped out, but I decided that I would finish. Hypothermia claimed at least seventy runners, and ambulances were stationed every mile. One man crossed the finish line, collapsed from hypothermia, and died of a heart attack. I thought through the entire race, *I can't do this, I can't do this.* It's more in your mind than in your body.

She finished! Not with the time she wanted, but she finished.

No wonder Paul says that the Christians at Corinth "gave themselves first to the Lord" (2 Corinthians 8:5). Jesus calls us to finish the race. There's an unconditional quality about it: Keep running regardless with your eyes on Jesus; don't look back, but do relinquish anything that weighs you down. If you have to pause, stop for nourishment, support, or forgiveness, but don't quit the race! You can make it, because the end is near.

Joe Almanza knows something about perseverance. His early life was one of crime. He tells how his daddy took him and his brothers into a motel room in Mexico and dumped out on the bed large suitcases filled with money. It was money he had made as a chief of drug traffic in an area in Mexico. He was teaching Joe and his brothers how to make money by trafficking in drugs.

Joe learned his lesson well from his daddy. He spent seven years in the Texas prison system. He could have come out of that prison as heir to drug traffic with literally millions of dollars, but while in prison he met Jesus Christ. Jesus called to Joe, "Follow me," and Joe decided to become a Christian. He decided to put teeth in the song "I Have Decided to Follow Jesus." Today Joe dedicates himself to sharing Jesus with others, especially inmates. God voted for Joe, and Joe voted for God.

I have been with Joe in Huntsville, Texas, sitting on a concrete floor with him outside a jail door. I've watched him make contact with a man on the other side of that door. Sometimes he spoke Spanish, and I couldn't understand it all, but I watched Joe and listened. I noticed how quickly he got to the story of Jesus, rather than dwelling on idle chit chat. He immediately said, "I want to talk to you about Jesus, and we're here to stay as long as we need to stay."

I've seen Joe take the Bible to share Jesus Christ with many inmates. Joe converted his own brother, as well as the warden where he was serving. He's one of the very few men allowed in certain sections of the Texas prison system, because he is so trusted as a Christian. He's faithful to God, because he has decided to follow Jesus. He's finishing the race and keeping his promise.

The greatest promise you'll ever make is when you vow to follow Jesus . . . "no turning back, no turning back."

Thinking It Through

Opening Your Heart

This chapter stresses that "Christianity is a personal commitment."

- Why did Jesus make His religion so *personal?*
- How would you describe "personal commitment"?

Digging Into God's Word

Turn to Acts chapters 9, 22, and 26 for three stories of Paul's conversion. Notice that chapters 22 and 26 are Paul's own accounts of his commitment to Christ.

- How did Paul become a Christian?
- Describe the way in which Paul stresses the personal aspects of his conversion.
- What were some of the life-changing results in his life?

Taking It Home

To keep from performing only when it is convenient, here are several practical questions to assist you.

- What will your goal be this month if you are to personally close the distance between you and Jesus?
- How well are you running the race of life? At home? At work? With other people?
- Is there still something within your heart that you need to give up to be *totally* committed to Christ?

Chapter 3
Out of the Masses

Kerri Strug knew that the whole world had their eyes focused on her at that moment. In the language of gymnastics, she didn't "stick it" on her landing, because just as she came over the vault, she felt a searing pain in her ankle and leg. Would she try one more time? Or would she allow the injury to keep her from trying again? Kerri reached deep down into her gym bag of courage and commitment, and the rest is Olympic history as she became the heroine of the 1996 Olympics in Atlanta. Her jump on an injured leg led the U.S. women's gymnastic team to a gold medal. She kept the promise she had made to herself.

Can One Person Make A Difference?

- Our world was thought to be flat until Magellan sailed *around* it.

- Our world was filled with contagious diseases until a Frenchman named Pasteur inoculated it.

- Our world had no Bibles to read until Gutenberg invented his printing press.

- Our world lived in darkness until Thomas Edison flipped on the light.

- Our world was sick and didn't know effective nursing until Florence Nightingale came along.

- Our world was not religiously free until Martin Luther nailed his objections to the door of the church building and suffered for his convictions.

- America was not politically free until Thomas Jefferson led the way in signing the Declaration of Independence.

- America was not declared racially free until Abraham Lincoln initiated the Emancipation Proclamation.

- Our world did not know great music until five-year-old Mozart began playing with such God-given genius.

- Our world thought the sun revolved around the earth until Copernicus established the astronomical system of planets and stars.

Yes, one committed person makes an enormous difference in our world. Not only does history teach us this, but the Bible illustrates this principle with thrilling stories of real people.

Think about Moses. Here was a guy who wanted nothing to do with crowds or public speaking. But when he allowed God to use him, he became the greatest leader of God's people of all time. He rescued about two million of his people from slavery in Egypt. He delivered God's Law from Mt. Sinai to the people. This one self-conscious man guided God's people safely through the wilderness for over forty years and right up to the Promised Land. Wouldn't you say he made a difference? How? He kept his promises.

And who, except God himself, will ever know the real impact of the apostle Paul? This one man wrote over half of the New Testament, much of it from a prison cell. He preached most of the sermons recorded in the Bible, and he jarred the Roman Empire from center to circumference with the Good News of Jesus. Paul, one physically impaired man, spearheaded the evangelism of the Greco-Roman world, and his impact still reaches into our lives. This one man made an enormous difference for you and me because he stepped out of the masses and was faithful to his commitment to God.

Every Person Counts

It is easy today to be deceived into thinking that *"I don't count."* We're being coerced into believing that philosophy on every level of our culture and misled into believing that we can't make a real difference because we're simply part of the masses. We're moved around *en masse* by mass transportation. We're told what to do by mass media, and the products we need to survive are made by mass production. Like ignorant cattle, we allow ourselves to be herded, driven, grazed, watered, and even stampeded at the discretion of others.

A recent study of college-age people, or the X-Generation as they are sometimes called, showed that many of them are giving up. They think they have no hope and don't feel significant because they've been told over and over that they don't make any difference. They hear it at school, on television, and from the government. They are told daily that the only way to count is to be a part of a larger group—to join the masses.

I remember collecting final exams from my class at UCLA when a student stopped at my desk and quietly thanked me for knowing his name. "In four years at the university, you're the first professor ever to know my name. Other professors just know me by my I.D. number."

We're all known by our numbers these days. For instance, when we cash checks, they want numbers—driver's license numbers, credit card numbers, and phone numbers. When we interview for jobs, they want numbers—social security numbers, past employers' phone numbers, past salary numbers. On and on it goes as significance decays into insignificance.

The world says that we should not lift our heads above the masses—never do anything outstanding, never have any ambition, never accomplish anything important, never do anything particularly well. We're supposed to just stay in our places . . . *en masse.* Don't rock the boat; don't stand out; and don't be an individual; just follow the masses.

In contrast, Jesus says in Matthew 7:13, 14 that we shouldn't follow the masses, or the *many*, because they're headed in the wrong direction: "Enter through the narrow gate. For wide is the gate and broad is the road that leads to destruction, and *many* enter through it. But small is the gate and narrow is the road that leads to life, and only a *few* find it" (emphasis mine). It sounds to me as if stepping out of the masses is the best decision!

Controlled by Circumstances

Do you control circumstances, or do circumstances control you? Are you a victim or a victor of life? Here are some of those troublesome circumstances and what the Bible says about them:

Age. On the one hand, young people are being told that they are too young to count. Yet, the Bible says ". . . remember your Creator in the days of your youth" (Ecclesiastes 12:1). Do not despise your youth.

On the other hand, older people are told that *they* are too old to count. They hear, "You can't get a job, and you don't have any vitality because you're over sixty-five." Yet, God says that elders in the church are not to be novices. He instructs older women to teach younger women, and he says that gray hair is to be honored. The Word of God definitely teaches that age isn't a circumstance to keep us from feeling significant. We do count with God, no matter what age we are, from babies to seniors.

Gender. Women often feel frustrated that there is seemingly nothing significant for them to do in the church, that the entire church is male-operated and male-driven. They feel as if they don't count. But the first people to see Jesus on the day of His resurrection were women (Matthew 28:8-10). Phoebe was a special servant in the church at Rome (Romans 16:1). Paul gives special greetings to several prominent women in the church at Rome (Romans 16:3-16). Lydia became the first Christian on the European continent (Acts 16:11-15), and so many others could be listed. Gender is never an issue of acceptance or worth with Christ. There are different roles for men and women to play in the church, but in Christ Jesus, male and female work side by side to extend the kingdom of God.

Race. Our culture also tells some of us that we don't count because of the color of our skin. Even some churches have refused communion and worship to some because of their race. Some churches are up to their steeples in racism, but the Word of God teaches specifically that each person has equal significance to God, regardless of ethnic or racial origin.

When Claudius ordered all the Jews to leave Rome (Acts 18:2), he practiced ethnic cleansing, yet God continued to show special favor to the much hated Jews. And of course, the Jews hated non-Jews, so God had to confront Peter with his own racism. And Peter got the message: "I now realize how true it is that God does not show favoritism but accepts men from every nation who fear him and do what is right" (Acts 10:34). It seems God also made a special effort to save the Ethiopian (Acts 8:26f).

Racists demand that races be separated from one another. But "here there is no Greek or Jew, circumcised or uncircumcised, barbarian, Scythian, slave or free, but Christ is all and is in all" (Colossians 3:11).

Financial status. People often feel insignificant because they don't have much money. Yet, the Bible repeatedly reveals that finances are not related to personal worth or significance. It is the poor widow giving her last mite (half-cent) who was praised by Jesus and got the affirmation of the kingdom. It is not the rich man, but the poor beggar at his gate who went to heaven. However, some very rich people were also deeply involved in the kingdom of God, such as Abraham and David who were godly leaders of God's people. And Solomon, God's wise one, was proclaimed the wealthiest man in the world. You don't have to be able to count your money to count with God.

Culture also tells us that our health, physical appearance, jobs, and views of life are all factors that may control our lives and make us insignificant. Even our religion can be considered demeaning by our culture. And, yet, God discounts all these circumstances as accurate measures of our worth to Him. Sometimes the less significant we are to the world, the more significant we are to the kingdom, for it's no secret that God's yardstick is vastly different than the world's.

People who are midgets in the world may be giants in the kingdom, and giants in the world may not even exist in the kingdom. God had one Son, and He was not listed on Rome's top ten list of important people.

God Says We Do Count

Christianity shouts that a single person is important and that individual people do count. The shout comes in three different voices, each of which is important.

First, God teaches us that we can count and make a major difference in the world by putting our beliefs into action. "In the same way, faith by itself, if it is not accompanied by action, is dead" (James 2:17). "You see that a person is justified by what he does and not by faith alone" (James 2:24). When I put my beliefs into action, then my beliefs count. I make a difference when I walk my talk.

"Dear children, let us not love with words or tongue but with actions and in truth" (1 John 3:18). Let's not just preach sermons on love, but let's put our love into action. Let's not just claim to be committed to Christ, but let's put that commitment into action. James said that just saying you believe is dead belief. Just claiming to be committed to the kingdom is dead commitment. It is only by your actions that people know your faith and commitment. As the old adage says, "You can't plow a field by turning it over in your mind."

Most of us know that when we reach crossroads in our lives, these are the times we will always remember. They are emotional and mental hitching posts. Often we are the only ones there, and we must decide to stand by what we believe. We must live up to our own commitments. That's what makes these moments significant. Lech Walensa says, "The actual transformation of our convictions and beliefs into actions is a difficult path. The thing that lies at the foundation of positive change, the way I see it, is service to a fellow human being."

Why do historians write about Martin Luther? It's not because he was of German descent or because he was a Catholic. It's not because he was a priest or a really nice guy. It's because he stood at the Diet of Worms and said, "Here I stand. God so help me." The Pope excommunicated Luther from the Catholic church and began persecuting him. That was a major crossroads in his life. He stood up when he was the only person in that region of Germany who was going to do it. He stood alone, face-to-face with death and persecution, toe-to-toe with fear, and he refused to flinch. Such are the times when we put our beliefs into action, when commitment is either true or false, when promises are kept or not.

One of my teachers, Ira North, said, "The surest way to be lost is to do nothing." The parable of the talents illustrates this truth. The five-talent man went out and made five more talents. The two-talent man put his faith into action and made two more. But the one-talent man did nothing. He didn't lose his talent, but he didn't multiply it either. Our Lord didn't say to him, "Well you were a little too cautions, but maybe you'll do better next time." No. Jesus gave him one of the most scathing denunciations in all of Scripture because doing nothing equals faithlessness. Not running with the ball when it's handed off to you is the same as being tackled. You simply can't "do nothing" and win.

Jesus has the same problem with the barren fig tree. Jesus wasn't upset because it produced *bad* figs. He was angry because the tree just didn't produce anything at all, even though it was evidently capable of doing so. Jesus didn't say, "Well, let's baby it a little more, let's put some Miracle-Grow on it, let's transplant it and hope for the best." He said, with firmness in His voice, "Cut it down!" The plant didn't live up to its potential. It didn't do what it could do. It did nothing, and that was completely unacceptable to Christ.

The problem in the good Samaritan story is not that the priest and Levite came over and kicked the man in the face when he was down. No. They just walked by and did nothing. They didn't live up to their commitments as proclaimed men of God. They didn't step out of the masses and stand up for their beliefs. As Ira said, the surest way to be lost is to just never put your belief into action.

Second, God says that we do count and that we can make a difference by using our God-given gifts. We have different gifts according to the grace given us. If a man's gift is prophesying, let him use it in proportion to his faith. If it is serving, let him serve; if it is teaching, let him teach; if it is encouraging, let him encourage; if it is contributing to the needs of others, let him give generously; if it is leadership, let him govern diligently; if it is showing mercy, let him do it cheerfully. (Romans 12:6-8)

"There are different kinds of spiritual gifts, but the same Spirit . . . Now to each one the manifestation of the Spirit is given for the common good" (1 Corinthians 12:4, 7). When you became a Christian, God gave you His Holy Spirit—the gift of the Spirit (Acts 2:38)—so that you could use your ability for the common good. Paul said that the common good is for the welfare of the church, to build up the body of Jesus Christ: ". . . to prepare God's people for works of service, so that the body of Christ may be built up until we all reach unity in the faith and in the knowledge of the Son of God and become mature, attaining to the whole measure of the fullness of Christ" (Ephesians 4:12, 13).

"And in the church God has appointed first of all apostles, second prophets, third teachers, then workers of miracles, also those having gifts of healing, those able to help others, those with gifts of administration, and those speaking in different kinds of tongues" (1 Corinthians 12:28). God is the one who graciously gives to us.

John Wooden is the former UCLA basketball coach who led the Bruins to ten national championships in twelve years. I first met coach Wooden in 1963, and we still correspond as friends, because he is one my personal heroes. His first championship team actually came from what was affectionately termed the "B.O. Barn" because of the odor in the gym. There were no private lockers and no private showers. Players had to climb three flights of stairs to get to the gym. It had only two baskets. Coach Wooden helped the managers mop and sweep the floor every afternoon before practice.

Wooden says, "You could have written a long list of excuses why UCLA shouldn't have been able to produce a good basketball team there." Yet, the B.O. Barn gave birth to both the 1963 and 1964 national championship teams. Here's Wooden's take on it: "You must take what is available and make the very most of it."

That is especially true of the gifts or talents given by God to you and me. He gives gifts to youth; others are given to the aged. Some are public talents, such as preaching, singing, teaching, and leading prayer, while others are private gifts, such as counseling and listening. Some gifts are academic; some are practical. Some are moneyed and some are not moneyed. Specially gifted people are appointed as elders. Some with self-appointed gifts take the initiative. The Word of God is filled with examples of these gifts: Dorcas sewed, Phoebe ministered, Aquila and Priscilla were mobile missionaries. Churches chose deacons to serve widows while the apostles preached the Word. God said that we can make a difference by using our spiritual talents and gifts and being committed to the lives God has planned for us. He wants us to take what is available and make the very most of it.

Committed to a Cause

Third, we can make a difference when we become involved in something greater than ourselves. Paul stresses this: "It was he who gave some to be apostles, some to be prophets, some to be evangelists, and some to be pastors and teachers, to prepare God's people for works of service, so that the body of Christ may be built up until we all reach unity in the faith and in the knowledge of the Son of God and become mature, attaining to the whole measure of the fullness of Christ" (Ephesians 4:11-13). "From him the whole body, joined and held together by every supporting ligament, grows and builds itself up in love, as each part does its work" (Ephesians 4:16).

One of the magnificent teachings of the Bible is that we are not only gifted, but we are to be passionate. We are to put our heart into our promises. I don't think you can be successful in any venture without passion or enthusiasm. Boredom and apathy fill our world, and passion daily evaporates. Look at our culture—the suicide rate is high, depression is epidemic, addictions are rampant, people are bored, tranquilizers fill medicine cabinets. Yet, life was never meant to be despair. Even with all the diseases, accidents, and tragedies of life, you and I are called by Christ to give our hearts to a higher cause, to turn our eyes up, and to focus on God's providential movement. Heaven still touches earth, because when we feel His hands around us, we experience hope, forgiveness, and security. About that we can be passionate.

In 1990, I first met Igor Egirev in Rostov-on-Don in southern Russia. The Berlin Wall had just come down, and the world took a quick turn. Things would never again be the same in Russia. Igor would be a part of that revolution. As a Soviet engineer, Igor wondered what his future might be. Little did he know! One of the very first Russian Bibles to come into Russia after the fall of the Wall reached Igor. Carefully, analytically, and quickly, he began to read of Jesus, and Jesus turned out to be more than a myth or a mystery. He turned out to be Igor's Lord and Savior. Igor responded with passion to Jesus Christ, left his position with a Soviet firm, and committed himself to full-time ministry to his own people. Now the pulpit minister of the Rostov-on-Don church, Igor leads in serving orphans, the old, the hurting, and the disillusioned. Even the local authorities admire his commitment and his service. Passion in action—that's Igor Egirev in the new Russia.

Let's Make a Difference!

In a world of huge problems, in a culture that yawns with boredom, in cities that live on the fast track, in a system that caters only to the masses, *you can make a difference!* Here's how:

Element 1: Care Deeply. In order to make a real difference in any given area of life, we must care deeply about people. We must put our commitments into action. We must care enough about the cause and the people that we *"can't do nothing"* to help. We must find ourselves compelled to be involved, to stand up and be counted, to step out from the masses and take our places in the front line where the action is.

When we care enough about a cause and people, we won't have to be dragged forward into the fray; they'll have to hold us back. We won't have to be begged and reminded to do our part; they'll have to ask us to back off. It reminds me of the Israelites having to be asked to *stop* bringing their offerings to God because they had brought too much. That's what we should be guilty of in God's service. That's how strong our commitment should be.

Element 2: Work Hard. There are no easy ways to make a real difference in life. In studying American history we learn that in 1850, Daniel Webster gave the greatest speech of his life before the U.S. Senate. In his reply to Hayne, Webster skillfully argued for the union and its preservation.

Upon completion, reporters rushed up to him and asked, "How long had you worked on that speech?"

Webster answered, "I have been working on that speech all of my life."

Historians noted that his speech postponed the beginning of the Civil War by two full years. It took a lifetime of hard work and commitment to bring him to this point. But when it was time to step up to the plate, he hit a home run. Webster made a difference!

Element 3: Dare to Risk. In order to make a true difference, we must dare to take risks. Esther knew what it meant to take risks. She knew that if King Xerxes lowered his scepter, she would be killed, but she felt that she was born for just such a risky time. More than that, she was committed to save her people. So she said, "If I perish, I perish" (Esther 4:16b). Then she went in to the king, risking everything, and she succeeded in saving her people. That's total commitment in action. No easy answers. No magic push buttons. No short cuts. Esther didn't beat herself; she prepared for the risk. Then she took it and made an enormous difference.

Paul said that we should look at his record of risks (2 Corinthians). He suffered many hardships for the cause of Christ. Those hardships scared him, beat him, and left him for dead. But Paul was committed for the long haul. He ran the risk, and he certainly made the difference he wanted to make.

Do you remember Dietrich Bonhoeffer who risked his life in speaking out against the Nazis? Before the Nazis executed him, Bonhoeffer said, "Action springs not from thought, but from a readiness for responsibility." We remember Bonhoeffer, because he made a difference. But can you name the commander in chief who killed him?

Holiness and the ultimate goal of heaven are our rewards for faithfulness and commitment. You can make a difference, so step out of the masses and be counted, live up to your promises.

"I am only one, but still I am one;
I cannot do everything, but still I can do something;
because I cannot do everything,
I will not refuse to do the something I can do."
　　　　　　　　　　　　—Edward Everett Hale

Thinking It Through

Opening Your Heart

Jesus knows that you can make a difference, but in today's world we often think that one person doesn't count.

- How are you unique from any other person?
- Why do you think God made you special and unique?
- Give one example of when one person made a real difference.

Digging Into God's Word

Turn to Romans 16 where Paul mentions the names of Roman Christians who have made a real difference.

- Which of these people stands out to you personally? Why?
- Describe that person's special contributions to Christianity.

Taking It Home

In order to come "out of the masses," you can do some very important things and make a significant difference!

- Name a cause about which you care deeply. How can you personally advance it?
- How can you reach out to help someone who will not be able to help you in return?
- During the next month, make a list of every God-given talent you have. Use each ability in some way to help another person or cause that is important to you.

Chapter 4
Why Is Whole Religion So Hard to Sell?

The Dallas Morning News Religion Section of June 8, 1996, carried an article entitled "What's In A Name?" which presented a really tough problem:

> Jennifer Lee is a church-going woman with two children in Sunday school and a third just baptized at the First Congregational Church of San Jose, California. She believes in the divinity of Jesus Christ and has a lively interior dia-

logue with God. But she doesn't talk much about her Christian faith in public "because I'm afraid someone will think I'm a fundamentalist. . . . When I hear someone say something like, 'I am a Christian,' it makes my skin crawl."

The remainder of the article was about the word *Christian.* Today we have Christian bookstores, Christian telephone directories, Christian doctors, Christian schools, Christian singers, and an endless parade of Christian this and that. The word *Christian,* as the article pointed out, is used in a wide variety of ways. But isn't Jennifer's response interesting? It's probably typical, and it's probably fashionable in the lives of many people who claim to follow Jesus Christ and are members of some particular religious group to think of Christianity as something they don't want to talk about in public. To say "I am a Christian" today may, in fact, drive many people away.

Why is whole religion so hard to sell? People who work full time for a church or in Christian education are asked, "What do you do for a living?" That's an interesting question, and there are a variety of ways to answer it. When I'm introduced to someone as a minister, I sometimes see the negative expressions of those people, listen to their disgruntled mumblings, and watch them depart my presence as quickly as possible! I begin to feel like a modern-day leper.

Why Is the Christian Religion So Hard to Sell?

I recently asked a Jewish friend, "Why do so few Jews go to synagogue or keep Passover?"

"I guess," he quickly said, "it's because a lot of people are not interested in religion."

He may be right . . . perhaps more right than we would want to admit. We live in an age of disbelief. The problem of faith is the crucial problem of our times. The material, visible, experiential world so controls our lives and thoughts that only the most searching people seem willing to look beyond what meets the eye. Our senses are filled with the violent, sensual, crass, and selfish so that faith in God seems out of reach. We've gone to the bank of faith given by previous generations, withdrawn so often for our own purpose without making any deposits of our own, that we face bankruptcy.

While many people accept God in some sense, they have no personal relationship with Jesus. Unwilling to investigate His claims of divinity, they live life as though Jesus never lived. It reminds me of Thomas' struggle to have faith in Jesus: "Except I shall see the nail marks in his hands and put my finger where the nails were, and put my hand into his side, I will not believe it" (John 20:25). Thomases today still struggle.

TV magazine shows, popular magazines, and daily newspapers frequently carry stories of accusations against the divinity of Jesus. Some students of the Bible, armed with literary criticism, have thrown rocks at the authenticity of the text of Scripture. That God could have written the Bible is laughable to them. Perhaps writers like Paul were inspired much like Shakespeare to give us fresh human insight into the journey of mankind. Even some church leaders have come to believe that Jesus was neither sovereign nor divine. To believe in the text is to accept what some call the "myths" of Scripture. So how could this religion demand total commitment? Whole religion is hard to sell.

We might also conclude that we Christians are rather inadequate people, except for one important fact—Jesus himself found whole religion very difficult to sell to people. Maybe it's not the person selling it. Maybe it's the nature of *whole* religion—the kind of religion that Christianity really is, the kind that encompasses all of life. Maybe that's what keeps it from having a popular appeal to people, for whole religion is not always politically correct! What would happen if everybody in your neighborhood, in your office, in your class, or in your school, discovered that you were a Christian?

I remember a young man from Seattle who, claiming to be a Christian, went to work one summer as a lumberjack in Canada. When he returned home, some of his friends gathered around him and asked, "How did you make it up there? We heard some of those guys can really cuss and drink. They're really not followers of God. They use His name a lot, but it's usually in cursing."

He responded, "Well, in the three months I was there, they never learned I was a Christian."

God, on the other hand, dreams of an all-encompassing religion:

> One of the teachers of the law came and heard them debating. Noticing that Jesus had given them a good answer, he asked him, "Of all the commandments, which is the most important?" "The most important one," answered Jesus, "is this: 'Hear, O Israel, the Lord our God, the Lord is one. Love the Lord your God with all your heart and with all your soul and with all your mind and with all your strength.' The second is this: 'Love your neighbor as

yourself.' There is no commandment greater than these." "Well said, Teacher," the man replied. "You are right in saying that God is one and there is no other but him. To love him with all your heart, with all your understanding and with all your strength, and to love your neighbor as yourself is more important than all burnt offerings and sacrifices." When Jesus saw that he had answered wisely, he said to him, "You are not far from the kingdom of God." (Mark 12:28-34a)

The kind of religion Jesus describes is not part-time. It is not simply lived on Sunday for one hour. You can't clean it up for church and then act a different way at work or at school. Rather, it is *whole* religion, involving your whole life.

Jesus knows the only religion that really works in our lives is whole religion. Paul describes such total commitment when he says, "I die daily" (1 Corinthians 15:31). Whatever grips your heart—applause, ambition, pleasure, money—wants to rule you. Christ wants to rule you, too! His rule calls for daily death to anything that would challenge His authority over your life. "If anyone comes to me and does not hate his father and mother, his wife and children, his brothers and sistersflyes, even his own life—he cannot be my disciple" (Luke 14:26). Tough words! No, startling, horrible words!

Is Jesus really saying that to follow Him, we must "hate" our parents? "Hate" is a monstrous word, and clearly, Jesus teaches us to honor, provide, and respect our families. So what does "hate" mean? According to *The Abingdon Bible Commentary,* the root word means "to love less." *The Interpreter's Bible* claims that the word carries the idea of acting "as if" one hated his family, if the claims of the family ever conflicted with the claims of Christ. He calls for total commitment, undivided loyalty, complete allegiance. His hyperbole exaggerates the contrast for purposes of reaching our hearts. He wants supreme devotion because He knows that we make daily choices based on our feelings, emotions, and what is pleasing to others. He doesn't call for perfection but for faithfulness—yet it's still tough!

Obedience is not legalism. Rather it is the essence of the true relationship you have with a Lord who rules you. I've noticed over the years that some Christians accept Jesus as Savior because they feel the guilt of their sins. They want a Savior and gladly accept Him as Savior. But they balk at the idea of accepting Him as Lord. A lord rules you, controls you, exercises dominion and power over you, challenges any other power that wants to control you. So at a time when Caesar was proclaimed as Lord, Paul shouted, "That if you confess with your mouth, 'Jesus is Lord,' and believe in your heart that God raised him from the dead, you will be saved" (Romans 10:9).

Here is the crunch: We want Jesus as Savior, but not as Lord. Secretly, we want to stay in control of our lives. We don't want anyone telling us what to do. Fiercely independent, we want to "pull ourselves up by our own boot straps." It is almost like everyone else doesn't count! We climb the corporate ladder, which usually means we climb on and over a bunch of other folks. The culture routinely reminds us that "you are number one," and "you can have it all." But that reminder is alien to the teachings of Jesus. He consistently tells us that we make a choice everyday on how we will use His money, His time, His world, His treasures. "A servant of God," wrote Oswald Chambers, "is one who has given up forever his right to himself and is bound to his Lord as his slave."

We call each other *Christians*. We talk about Christian families, Christian music, and Christian values. But God only uses the word *Christian* three times in the Bible. When we look at each one of the times that He uses the word, it will tell us something about the nature of whole religion and why God wants it to demand your total commitment—heart, soul, understanding, and mind.

Christians Are Changed People

When the church was new, God wrote regarding a group of people who met in the city of Antioch: "The disciples were first called Christians at Antioch" (Acts 11:26). That is the first time the word *Christian* appears in the Bible. For eleven chapters, the New Testament church had been in existence and moved across Palestine and other parts of the Mediterranean Basin. Clearly, a people movement as a subset of Judaism would have hardly been noticed by the Roman government. When Luke described believers in Antioch, what did his use of the word *Christian* tell us? What did it say about whole religion?

First, it tells us that whole religion is hard to sell because it involves *change.* These believers at Antioch were *changed people.* There had been a turnaround in their lives. Outsiders could see that they were like Jesus Christ and not like they once were. They were enough like Christ to be called *Christians,* and their behavior, focus, meaning, and loyalty were all changed into His image. The Holy Spirit is given as a deposit within us so that we can begin to change. But some people don't want to change. Christianity really isn't for them, because Christ is never satisfied with people who are satisfied with the status quo and with themselves.

God loves positive changes in our lives. He authors them and commands them. In John 3 he talks about a *new birth*. In Romans 6 he talks about a *new life*. Christianity is based upon the premise that we can change. We cannot change ourselves, but Jesus Christ can change us. God invented the "c" word—change, change, change. Change is a process. It is an active, ongoing, sometimes slow, necessary, step-by-step journey. God is not interested in status quo, excuses, rigidity, or blaming others. To be a *Christian* is to change. That's what Christianity demands. It calls for us to never be satisfied with our lives, for us to constantly be making changes in our lives.

Can you name some turning points in your life? The day or the night you became a Christian was a turning point. Maybe a simple but meaningful conversation changed your life. It may have been a trip to Russia or to the Holy Land. It may have been an emergency in the middle of the night. Each time the telephone rings at 2 A.M., it is most likely a turning point in someone's life. An accident. A death. An emotional disaster.

There are points when we change, points when we put our beliefs into action. But Jesus Christ calls for radical, comprehensive change. They were called *Christ*-ians because they changed their lives to be like Jesus Christ.

Christians Make Choices

Paul had just finished preaching a sermon about Jesus Christ to a ruler named Agrippa. Then he became bold. He put before Agrippa the choice of whether or not to become a Christian himself.

Agrippa said to Paul, "Do you think that in such a short time you can persuade me to be a Christian?" (Acts 26:28). Agrippa was facing a choice, and he was going to remember that day because he made a deliberate choice.

Paul replied, "Short time or long—I pray God that not only you but all who are listening to me today may become what I am, except for these chains." I hope you will choose, Agrippa, to become a follower of Jesus Christ and to confess His name and be baptized into Christ. The story presents a different and new insight into the meaning of *Christian.*

Whole religion may be hard to sell because it involves difficult choices. In his book entitled *Odyssey*, John Scully wrote of his career decision to move from being the president of PepsiCo to the president of Apple Computer. Scully said it was one of the toughest decisions of his life.

Steve Jobs finally asked him, "Do you want to spend the rest of your life selling sugared water, or do you want a chance to change the world?"

Scully commented, "The question was a monstrous one—one for which I had no answer. It simply knocked the wind out of me."

You see, there are times in our lives when we face choices. They are the forks in the road, and the road we take determines everything. When faced with his fork in the road, poet Robert Frost said, "I took the one less traveled, and that has made all the difference."

When Christianity began, the name *Christian* may have been a positive description or at least a neutral one. But by the end of the first century, the choice to become a *Christ*-ian was not a simple one, because the name itself was one of derision. Critics, troublemakers, and enemies of Christ's followers called them *Christ*-ians. It was a put-down, a slur, a mud-slinging attempt to discredit them. So making the choice to wear the name *Christian* was choosing to be an outcast of society, a rebel against the government, one disowned by family and friends. It was choosing Jesus Christ above everything and everybody else in life—a total commitment . . . for life, forever.

After we become Christians, every day we choose between ourselves and Jesus. Do I choose to become a *new* person as a Christian or just a *nicer* person? Do I choose to be unique and different in school or to conform? Do I choose my religion out of duty or out of desire? Am I really responsible as a Christian, or am I just half-hearted in my effort? Am I saying "no" to myself, or am I saying that everything is permissible? Am I saying "yes" to justice or to injustice? Am I really committed to Christ or not?

My experience says to me that Christian choices take longer than non-Christian choices. They require more thought and prayer and they are more difficult. Here are some questions you might want to ask yourself as you make choices in your own life. You're faced with a fork in the road. You're a believer, but being part of whole religion involves choices, and you begin to ask questions like these:

- What would Jesus do if He were me?
- How will this affect my brothers and sisters in Christ?
- Will this draw me closer to Jesus Christ?

- How will this impact my influence as a Christian?
- What should be my proper behavior in the presence of God?

These are unsettling, disquieting, tough questions. It's much easier to "duck and run." But if you choose whole religion, you will become accustomed to them.

Christians Will Be Challenged

Before you put this book down, there's more. When Peter talked about suffering, he said, "If you suffer as a Christian, do not be ashamed, but praise God that you bear his name" (1 Peter 4:16). Whole religion is hard to sell for another reason—it involves *challenge*. Peter affirms that if we wear the name *Christian* there will be some challenges to our faith from the very day we become Christians. We say to new Christians, "Satan is coming after you this week. He will try to deceive you into thinking that your choice to follow Jesus Christ was the wrong choice, and you'll face Satan's challenge immediately."

Satan loves new Christians, because they are naive, inexperienced, changeable, putty in his satanic hands. He thinks he doesn't have to be too subtle with new babies. Subtlety is for old veteran Christians who recognize his techniques. He can be in the face of a new Christian and blast him before he knows what's hit him. Maybe he can take a new Christian down with one shot, one challenge, one deception.

You see, the bad news about new Christians is that they are new Christians. But the good news about new Christians is also that they are new Christians. There's something else about them besides the fact that they are new. They are also Christians. They have a new loyalty, love, and commitment. It was a private matter made public. They confessed Jesus as Lord and became Christians. Satan may try to knock a new Christian out, but now reinforcements have come for the war. God's Spirit now lives within them.

> Now we are the children of God (1 John 3:2).

> We know that we live in him and he in us, because he has given us of his Spirit (1 John 4:13).

> You, dear children, are from God and have overcome them, because the one who is in you is greater than the one who is in the world (1 John 4:4).

You may wonder what the Holy Spirit can really do for your life. There is more than one answer.

The Holy Spirit empowers you. When I lived in Los Angeles I remember seeing the transmission towers that would bring electrical power from the Colorado River into Los Angeles. They would break down the high voltage into usable units for homes like ours. The Holy Spirit breaks down the limitless power of God into usable units for your life. The power of God is unimaginable, dangerous, irresistible, and intense. But the Holy Spirit is your transformer who enables you to face adversity, suffering, and even persecution.

The Spirit prays for you. I remember my friend Walter Garretson describing his first prayer. His wife, Caroline, was extremely ill, and he got on his knees and prayed one word: "Help!" But the Spirit of God prayed for him. When the Holy Spirit speaks to God about you and me, His attention is totally on us. He speaks in a language we can't comprehend; we can't find any human expression for it. But He prays with empathy because He knows us so well. He prays with effectiveness because He knows what the Father wants for us. So He connects our needs with the desire of God.

The Holy Spirit intercedes for you. His intercession is based on His perfect knowledge of a new Christian's life. He also has perfect knowledge of God's loyal love and a perfect understanding of God's will. No wonder Paul said, "And he who searches our hearts knows the mind of the Spirit, because the Spirit intercedes for the saints in accordance with God's will" (Romans 8:27). Maybe one reason the first Christians devoted themselves to prayer was that they saw how the Holy Spirit deciphered their requests according to God's will and did more than they ever dreamed. No doubt, Stephen prayed that God would use him and his influence to impact others for Christ. So the Holy Spirit took Stephen's prayers and asked the Father to let him be stoned to death. As Stephen gave glory to God, Saul of Tarsus witnessed his martyrdom, and he never forgot it. It may have been the first genuine influence in the conversion of Saul.

To wear the name Christian in the first century could be quite costly. When the Emperor Trajan sent Pliny the Younger to Bithynia in A.D. 112, the subject of Christianity came up. In Pliny's letter to Trajan, he expressed uncertainty and doubt as to how to treat this new cult called Christianity.

> I was never present at any trial of Christians; therefore I do not know what are the customary penalties or investigations, and what limits are observed. I

have hesitated a great deal on the question whether there should be any distinction of ages; whether the weak should have the same treatment as the more robust; whether those who recant should be pardoned, or whether a man who has ever been a Christian should gain nothing by ceasing to be such; whether the name itself, even if innocent of crime, should be punished, or only the crimes attaching to that name.

Pliny then disclosed how dangerous the very name Christian had become by the end of the first century A.D. Clearly the Roman government no longer saw Christianity as simply a Jewish cult but as a dangerous enemy. To wear the name Christian meant total commitment. "I ask them if they are Christians. If they admit it I repeat the question a second and third time, threatening capital punishment; if they persist I sentence them to death."

The Romans arrested a very well known Christian minister by the name of Lucian. The Romans didn't waste much time with formalities. They asked Lucian only three questions before they killed him:

"Lucian, what is your name?" they asked him.

He replied in Latin, "I am Christian."

"Lucian, where are you from?"

He replied in Latin, "I am Christian."

"Lucian, what is your occupation?"

He replied in Latin, "I am Christian."

With that last statement they took off his head. Lucian, like many people, wore the name Christian proudly. Today you can visit the Roman Forum. But, when you visit, you must also go to the Circus Maximus. To Christians, the Circus Maximus is holy ground because more Christians died there than in the Roman Coliseum. Many of them died as Lucian did, saying, "I am a Christian."

What's in that name? It means *change, choice,* and *challenge.* It means commitment to finish the race. It means to love God with all your heart, with all your soul, and with all your mind. It means keeping your whole-hearted promises to God, His Son, and His Spirit.

Can you truly say that your religion is *whole* religion, or is it a religion with *holes?*

Thinking It Through

Opening Your Heart

God wraps up His notion of whole religion in one
word—Christian.

- What is your reaction to this?
- Can you think of other words to describe whole religion?

Digging Into God's Word

Turn to 1 Corinthians 15:31 and concentrate on the
phrase "I die every day."

- Since Paul did not physically die, what is he talking
  about?
- What is the relationship between submission/obedi-
  ence and allowing Christ to totally control your life?
- If Christians are changed people, what are the points
  of change?

Taking It Home

- If you are to personally make some new choices leading to greater commitment to wholehearted Christianity, what would they be?
- Is C.S. Lewis right in believing that wholehearted Christianity involves suffering?
- How do you sense God leading you into greater commitment?

Chapter 5
The Death of Trust

Recently the *Los Angeles Times* magazine asked this question: "Is Walter Cronkite the last trustworthy man in America?" If you are a teenager, Walter Cronkite may be a new name, but to those of us who have lived longer, that name represents one of the most famous newscasters in broadcasting. The image of Cronkite goes back twenty-five years to when pollsters found him to be the most trusted public figure in the United States. And even when Cronkite stepped down as the anchor of the *CBS Evening News* and Dan Rather took over, Walter Cronkite was still the most trusted television figure in the country.

"Cronkite has deep misgivings about the state of our country," maintains the *Los Angeles Times*, "that could be characterized as mistrust. He is critical of institutions like the press and the government and particularly the office of the President. He readily admits that he has lapsed from skepticism into cynicism."

Is it any wonder that men like Walter Cronkite are skeptical and cynical when articles of impeachment are delivered against the President of the United States? The scene was grave because of the seriousness of the allegations. On December 9, 1998, Charles F.C. Ruff presented the final defense on behalf of the White House against impeachment. Mr. Ruff, an experienced criminal lawyer and a Watergate special prosecutor, leaned forward in his wheelchair to speak to the House Judiciary Committee. He lowered his voice to dramatize the gravity of the moment. He hoped that Mr. Clinton could be rescued from becoming the only President other than Andrew Johnson to be impeached by the House. As the top lawyer for the President, Ruff concluded that "reasonable people" might decide that President Clinton had lied under oath. *"He misled his family, his friends, his colleagues and the public,"* said Mr. Ruff, *"and in doing so, he betrayed the trust placed in him not only by his loved ones but by the American people"* (*The New York Times*, December 10, 1998).

Everywhere we turn, trust is becoming a casualty. Alexis de Tocqueville reports in 1835 finding "tremendous trust" and a strong emphasis on personal integrity among Americans. Not long ago we could say that when a man gave you his word that it was his bond, but we have come a long way from "Honest Abe" . . . a long way the *wrong* way! "'There is no shame' anymore, says Jorja Prover, an anthropologist at UCLA's School of Public Policy and Social Research" (*Los Angeles Times*, November 11, 1998).

John P. Crossley, Jr., associate professor of religion at the University of Southern California, says, "The whole thing is tied up with the depersonalization of society. With society structured in an impersonal way, where you don't necessarily know the people you do business with, you can certainly break pledges more easily." Crossley cites that in 1900, four of ten Americans lived in urban centers. But today, seven of ten Americans live in urban areas, which "has made strangers of us within our own communities." His evidence proves that "personal integrity—the backbone of oath-keeping—once coursed more vigorously" in earlier America (*Los Angeles Times*, November 11, 1998).

Today, rather than a handshake of integrity, we have rampant litigation, piles of lawsuits, prenuptial agreements, and lots of fine print to define our relationships. We're past handshakes and into courtrooms. Politicians and legislators are public jokes.

In a *Los Angeles Times* article from November 11, 1998, Scott Martell writes:

> . . . there is a pervasive perception that the once-solemn vow—be it formal, with a hand on the Bible, or an informal personal pledge—doesn't carry the same depth of commitment that it used to. The aura of the oath, with its promise before God, has been deadened by ritual, some experts say. "'Til death do us part" lasts only a few years for many newlyweds. And a courtroom oath to "tell the whole truth" seems to carry an invisible asterisk: "Unless my lawyer tells me it'll make me look bad."

On April 13, 1981, Janet Cooke of the *Washington Post* was awarded a Pulitzer Prize for her moving account of an eight-year-old boy hooked on heroin. Just a few days later, her story was exposed as a fabrication. The Pulitzer Prize was returned, and the integrity of all journalism was called into question. Public trust died a little more that day.

Recently George Barna, in his research in Glendale, California, said that 36 percent of all Americans say that lying is sometimes necessary. Seventy-one percent of Americans expect lying and cheating to increase in the future. And more than one-third of all students say they would lie on their resume or a job application.

Federal judge Lacey A. Collier, commenting on her reason for imposing a 13-month prison sentence for perjury, states, "One of the most troubling things in our society today is people who raise their hands, take an oath to tell the truth and then fail to do that. An analogy might be made to termites that get inside your house. Nobody sees it, nobody knows about it until the house collapses around you" (*The New York Times*, November 17, 1998).

Darrell West, a professor at Brown University, says that "The rising level of mistrust is the most profound in public opinion over the last three decades. If you go back to the 1950s, about 70 percent trusted the government in Washington to do the right thing. Today about 70 percent mistrust the government. There is no other change," West concludes, "that is so dramatic."

Even contemporary ethicists are startled at the subtle shift away from absolutes to tolerance. For example, Rushworth Kidder, president of the Institute for Global Ethics in Camden, Maine, "says he is afraid that the decline of the oath is indicative of a broad cultural abandonment of personal ethics." He states that "even families, even churches, no longer emphasize the value of personal integrity—the result . . . of moral relativism. Tolerance 'is a wonderful concept,'" Kidder asserts. "But sometimes . . . tolerance of differences can expand unintentionally to tolerance of unethical acts" (*Los Angeles Times*, November 11, 1998).

Trust in the press, trust in our government, trust in some business institutions, trust in universities, seem to be at an all-time low. Recently pollster George Gallup found that even confidence in religion has taken quite a slide in the past twenty-five years with tele-evangelism and many other problems that have come upon churches. In the 1960s we heard, "Don't trust anybody over thirty." Today we hear a stronger version: "Don't trust anyone." I even saw a bumper sticker which read, "Be sincere, whether you mean it or not." Our culture has basically rejected the idea of absolute values. It now says there are no fixed standards to guide one's living. We have opted for situation ethics. Freud told us to throw away the Ten Commandments. We did. He said we'd be happy. We aren't. We're miserable and confused. There are more sex problems, broken families, and depression today than ever before. As Scripture says, it seems that now every man is doing "what is right in his own eyes" (Judges 17:6).

Trust in the Book

How do we revive trust when it seems so hopeless? Kidder points out that "People are afforded a lot more excuses. As a society, we have moved the line over in terms of what we are going to allow. We have become a society that appropriately recognizes that people are under stress and have conflicts and pressures that often make them lie and engage in behavior that is less than admirable" (*Los Angeles Times*, November 11, 1998).

Maybe there is hope! "We need a language of public discourse," says Kidder, "that lets us talk about these kinds of subjects in a robust, powerful and immediately relevant way. . . . In most [new media] stories, the undergirding conceptual framework is, 'Is this politically astute or economically viable?' not, 'Is this morally right?' We need to find the language to answer that question" (*Los Angeles Times*, November 11, 1998).

We can we find that language? Even though many people view the Bible as just another piece of data, could it be that it provides the very language that we are looking for? Listen to the trustworthy Word of the Lord:

- "Some trust in chariots and some in horses, but we trust in the name of the LORD our God" (Psalm 20:7).
- "But I trust in you, O LORD; I say, 'You are my God'" (Psalm 31:14).
- "Blessed is the man who makes the LORD his trust, who does not look to the proud, to those who turn aside to false gods" (Psalm 40:4).
- "Trust in him at all times, O people pour out your hearts to him, for God is our refuge" (Psalm 62:8).
- "Those who trust in the LORD are like Mount Zion, which cannot be shaken but endures forever" (Psalm 125:1).
- "Trust in the LORD with all your heart and lean not on your own understanding" (Proverbs 3:5).
- "Surely God is my salvation; I will trust and not be afraid. The LORD, the LORD, is my strength and my song; he has become my salvation" (Isaiah 12:2).
- "Put your trust in the light while you have it, so that you may become sons of light" (John 12:36).
- "May the God of hope fill you with all joy and peace as you trust in him, so that you may overflow with hope by the power of the Holy Spirit" (Romans 15:13).

Did you hear the theme, the advice and counsel from God's Book? In a time of false gods, manipulation, and the death of trust, we are to trust God and His Word. You can put your trust in Him, because He is your refuge and your strength. Recommit yourself to God, for trust and commitment depend on each other for strength and power.

God Knows that Trust Is Sacred

What does God want you to know about trust? When trust is on the defensive, when so many seem untrustworthy, when marriages break up, families dissolve, and responsibility seems so rare, what does God want us to realize?

He knows that truth, honor, and dependability spring from His nature. "Just and true are your ways" (Revelation 15:3). Trust is connected to who God is.

It is God who does not lie (Titus 1:2). Trust marks the Christian's commitment. Christians believe that personal integrity in their dealings must be at the highest level. You cannot deal in half-truths, deceptions, or character assassinations and be like God, because God is full of trust, integrity, and honor. God is the opposite to Satan. Truth is the opposite of deception. In fact, one of the strongest things our Lord says is this: "You belong to your father, the devil, and you want to carry out your father's desire. He was a murderer from the beginning, not holding to the truth, for there is no truth in him. When he lies, he speaks his native language, for he is a liar and the father of lies" (John 8:44).

Christ is saying that, if you look at His enemy, his whole nature is one of deception. You can't trust him. You can't believe Satan. His reputation is dishonesty, falsehood, deception. But if you deal with God, you are dealing with honor and integrity itself. You deal with someone who cannot lie for He is Truth. His very nature is trust.

Character: Our Most Important Possession

If trust and integrity have worked anywhere, it's been in our military academies. But not today. Cadets "are more cavalier toward the Cadet Honor Code ('We will not lie, steal, or cheat nor tolerate among us anyone who does')." According to Lieutenant Colonel Terrence Moore, U. S. Air Force Academy, "We've gotten away from the focus on the most common values that people share, things like integrity and selflessness, responsibility, decency, honesty—basic core values that everybody agrees on" (*The Dallas Morning News*, December 11, 1993). Pick a reason: MTV, liberal universities, media, leaders, whatever. We're in trouble!

We are slowly losing our character. We don't teach responsibility as we should; instead we teach explanations. If someone is caught cheating on an exam, instead of admitting it, he attempts to explain it away. We accept his explanation, because we don't want to be too harsh, and we call for tolerance. Over and over the Word of God says that our character is the most important possession we own. "A good name is far more desirable than great riches: to be esteemed is better than silver or gold" (Proverbs 22:1).

Aristotle said in *Rhetoric I,* "We believe good men more fully and more readily than others." He also said, "A speaker's character may almost be called the most effective means of persuasion that he possesses." Aristotle was right. A speaker's character, his credibility, is the most important persuasive element he has in his speaking repertoire. If the speaker is a person that's trusted, we believe anything he says, even when it's a little far-fetched. But if a speaker's character is questionable, we're suspicious of everything he says, even if it makes perfect sense. No wonder Quintilian defines a great speaker as "a good man speaking well."

Perhaps, no speaker was more trusted to lead the moment than Winston Churchill in 1940. Born November 30, 1874, in Oxfordshire, England, Churchill entered Sandhurst on his third attempt. The military was in his blood. He served as a war correspondent in 1895 in campaigns in Cuba. In India in 1897 and in the Sudan in 1898, he led forces as an officer. By 1911, Churchill became the First Lord of the Admiralty and directed the Royal Fleet at the beginning of World War I in 1914.

Between 1933 and 1939, he spoke out against the looming Nazi presence in Europe. Historian John Keegan wrote, "He stood out as the one man in whom the nation could place its trust." When Parliament gave Chamberlain a no-confidence vote, England turned to the man she most trusted—Winston Churchill.

As Prime Minister, Churchill said England "stood alone" after the Nazis defeated France. Next on Hitler's agenda was England, yet Churchill refused Hitler's offers of peace and prepared the nation for the Battle of Britain. As the most trusted leader of the English people, Churchill rallied them in one of his most famous speeches—his 1940 address to Parliament:

> I have, myself, full confidence that if all
> do their duty, if nothing is neglected . . .
> we shall prove ourselves once again able
> to defend our island home, to ride out the
> storm of war, and to outlive the menace of

tyranny, if necessary for years, if necessary alone. . . . Even though large tracts of Europe . . . have fallen or may fall into the grip of the Gestapo and all the odious apparatus of Nazi rule, we shall not flag or fail. We shall go on to the end, we shall fight in France, we shall fight on the seas and the oceans, we shall fight with growing confidence and growing strength in the air, we shall defend our island, whatever the cost may be, we shall fight on the beaches, we shall fight on the landing grounds, we shall fight in the fields and in the streets, we shall fight in the hills, we shall never surrender.

It was the greatest speech ever made by the most trusted speaker in the 20th century! By 1949, Winston Churchill would give his well-known victory sign to cheering crowds in Strasbourg, France. This most credible orator had rallied the democracies to a final triumph, and so the world spoke English, not German.

But since that monumental victory, integrity or credibility in some of our democratic leaders has waned. With the decline, we've trusted our leaders less and less. We just *thought* we knew them!

As we enter the 21st century, our values seem to become more cloudy as we bow more often before the "god of tolerance." As we lower the flag of absolute truth from the masthead of life, we sail off into treacherous waters. What a paradox! As America fought the Cold War with her values intact, she then grew less and less certain what those values ought to be. Surrounded by everything to live with, we have less and less to live for. Depression is "epidemic," claims the *Wall Street Journal*. Suicide claims our young and our old in record numbers. Trust dies.

Where do we start to find a solution? Politicians suggest sweeping changes in government and education, but maybe the solution is more personal. Maybe it starts with something as simple as giving your word and keeping it. Making a vow or a promise. When you give your word, it represents you, your character. The Bible uses the word *vow* to means serious promise, not to be taken lightly. It may be an expression of devotion to God (Psalm 22:25). But it's always as sacredly binding as your oath. So you find Jacob, Jephthah, Hannah (mother of Samuel), and Paul all made vows, and when they made their vows, they were putting their personal characters on the line.

Jesus, in His famous Sermon on the Mount, stresses the absolute necessity of keeping our personal word when we give it.

> Again, you have heard that it was said to the people long ago, "Do not break your oath, but keep the oaths you have made to the Lord." But I tell you, Do not swear at all: either by heaven, for it is God's throne; or by the earth, for it his footstool; or by Jerusalem, for it is the city of the Great King. And do not swear by your head, for you cannot make even one hair white or black. Simply let your "Yes" be "Yes," and your "No," "No"; anything beyond this comes from the evil one. (Matthew 5:33)

Jesus thinks our character is so crucial that when we give our word, we're giving our sacred trust, our bond. It's our honor code. We don't need to say, "I swear on a stack of Bibles" or "I take this oath on my mother's grave." We don't need to boost our words with props. Our integrity speaks for itself. No front, no neon, no glitz. Our reputation speaks more loudly than any wildly stated prop. When we say something, we mean it.

Parents are especially vulnerable on this point, it seems. Sometimes they say "no" to their child's request, but when the child continues to pester them about their refusal, they give in and change their answer to "yes" just to silence the child. But that's the very time the parents need to hold the line so that their child understands that "no" means "no." When it changes to "yes," their child is then confused and begins to believe the parents' word is not trustworthy. The result? He or she learns to mistrust the parents' word and promises, and the parents' character becomes questionable to their children. And long-range it results in the children's lack of character, because they pattern themselves after what they see their parents do.

Paul emphasized this when he wrote to a young man by the name of Timothy:

> Have nothing to do with godless myths and old wives' tales; rather, train yourself to be godly. For physical training is of some value, but godliness has value for all things, holding promise for both the present life and the life to come . . . Don't let

> anyone look down on you because you are
> young, but set an example for the believ-
> ers in speech, in life, in love, in faith and
> in purity. . . . Watch your life and doctrine
> closely. Persevere in them, because if you
> do, you will save both yourself and your
> hearers. (1 Timothy 4:7, 8, 12, 16)

Your credibility and character are your most important assets, especially when you are young. Watch
yourself closely—be more like God and less like those
who are untrustworthy. Be committed to maintaining
the characteristics of God himself. Paul was giving
strong, solid advice to a young man who was preparing
to preach. Yet, his advice is just as valuable today to
any young person, regardless of occupation.

Integrity: The Basis of Trust

How many times do you hear it? In marriage and
family counseling we hear it often. A lady makes an
appointment and comes to your office. You ask how you
can help her, and she starts crying and says, "I was
totally surprised when my husband left for another
woman. I couldn't have been more shocked. I didn't
have the slightest hint that anything at all was wrong

in our marriage. But he said he has been unhappy for years and now it's too late to save our marriage."

Even though they made a promise years ago for a life commitment for better or for worse, divorce becomes a very real option in the lives of people. But divorce results more from a process than a single event. Dr. D. R. Harvey has written in his book *Love Secured: How To Prevent A Drifting Marriage*, "Drifting is a gradual, subtle, often unintentional severing of the emotional ties between a husband and wife."

Having spent a lot of time in marriage and family counseling, my experience tells me that a single event does not usually cause divorce. It is a gradual ebbing away of trust over months and years. It starts at places like the water fountain at work or at lunch. It looks innocent in the beginning, because it is—just an exchange of looks and words over time. But after several conversations, a person steps over the invisible line of fidelity and goes too far. Finally, commitment is lost, the promise is broken, and integrity is violated.

It's tough to be married today. Couples can be overwhelmed by the demands of life. Many people today work seventy to eighty hours a week. Some catch a plane on Monday morning and return on Friday. There's an enormous exhaustion level with couples who rear children, especially when both parents work.

Success drives a growing number of us. Both partners are working to pay off debts and purchase a house. Slowly a husband and wife can begin to take each other for granted. Intimacy is broken, and drifting becomes accepted. The same is true in business dealings, school work, and family relationships. Integrity goes on the skid.

Even When Nobody's Looking

He's the most honest man I ever knew, and I knew him really well—he's my dad. Some of my most memorable whippings came when I had not told the whole truth. I watched him prepare his income tax return, and it was honest in every detail. He even submitted it early! Dad never used work supplies for projects at home. He insisted on exact detail, without exaggeration, in making reports to the U.S. Government or his employer. To my dad, lying was the worst sin because it broke faith, destroyed character, and ruined reputation. He was faithfully married to Mom for more than sixty years. Integrity to Dad was everything. If you had it, you could hit a home run in life. If you had money, education, and contacts, but no integrity, you'd never get to first base. That may be one reason the U.S. Postal Service gave him the assignment of working registered mail—the kind with actual money and negotiable paper in it. They knew he could be trusted, even when nobody was looking.

I guess that's why the pulpit minister at our family congregation, Batsell Barrett Baxter, used to come over so often and sit in the backyard confiding in Dad. He knew that Dad could be totally trusted. I guess that's why the elders of our church assigned so many money projects to Dad during the more than thirty years he served as an elder. They knew they could depend on his integrity, even when they weren't looking. Perhaps that's why so many young Christian businessmen and professionals in Nashville sought his counsel. And maybe that's why, even through tough times like World War II and Dad's struggle with tuberculosis, Mom and Dad's marriage lasted until death parted them. They were faithful to each other, even when nobody was watching. That's why my sister Linda and I talked to Dad about so many personal concerns. We knew we could trust him.

Dad knew that if you can't trust yourself, you can't expect others to trust you? He also knew that, when you think nobody else is looking, God is!

All the Time, or Not At All

We have experienced the death of trust when we have to go back twenty-six years to find the most trustworthy man in America. We must try to reverse that trend. Integrity begins with respect and reverence for God. Dallas business leader Todd Miller has written, "Restoring trust in our business community, indeed in our society as a whole, will occur only through a return to basic moral principles founded on a simple faith in a living God."

We must be people of integrity in our schools, in all of our business dealings at work, in our families, and in all of our relationships. We must be people of integrity when we make a promise and a commitment, in marriage and when we rear our children. We must be people of integrity when we live our lives from Mondays through Saturdays, as well as on Sundays in worship. In truth, we must be committed to truth and integrity all the time, or we're actually not committed to truth and integrity at all.

The Bible prohibits these three things: (1) telling a lie—because it ruins us and ruins others; (2) spreading a lie—gossip; and (3) living the lie. Scott Peck, in his book *People of the Lie,* describes people who cannot admit the possibility of any evil inside of them. Because they cannot admit it, they see no need for changing their lives. They decide that they didn't do anything wrong and refuse to change. At that point they are living the lie. They are not committed to truth when they can't tell themselves the truth.

Fakes and False Fronts

A number of years ago I had the opportunity to be on the set of *Gunsmoke* for two days. It was the number one TV western at the time. Bill Bramley, a character actor who always played either a terribly funny or a terribly mean role, was a personal friend of mine. He picked me up at 3:30 A.M. to take me to the set of *Gunsmoke*.

When I got in the car, he said, "Isn't this glamorous?"

I said, "No, it's sleepy. It's not glamorous."

When we arrived at the set of the famous Longbranch saloon where Matt Dillon, Miss Kitty, and Festus were playing a scene, it amused me to see that it was just a false front. There was no ceiling. The chandelier hung from one of the rafters. The walls of the Longbranch looked solid, but they weren't. Everything *looked* real, but it was only a series of false fronts and imitation sets.

Our world today is filled with false fronts and imitations. People look real, but they are often false. Situations look real and dependable, but they're fakes. Politicians promise one thing but do the reverse. Tele-evangelists use religion to promote their own agendas of power and greed.

God wants us to be the most trustworthy people on earth. He knows that trust is sacred. Your reputation and credibility are the most important things you possess. When you make a promise, live by that promise. God is looking for trust in a trustless age, and this is possible because Christ is totally trustworthy: "I am the way, and the truth and the life" (John 14:6), and "I can do all things through Christ who gives me the strength" (Philippians 4:13). Jesus is the only way to God, but He is totally dependable, and you can trust Him to keep His promise to lead you home. He is not a false front; He's the real thing. He's the trustworthy guide. He doesn't change with the times nor acclimate to the culture. He is the same loving, caring, compassionate, just Savior all the time.

The question is, *Can He trust you to keep your promise to follow Him all the way?*

Thinking It Through

Opening Your Heart

The evidence seems overwhelming that trust, integrity, and honor are on the defensive.

- What are some examples you can name of "the death of trust"?
- In your opinion, what are the reasons for the decline of trust?

Digging Into God's Word

Turn to 1 Timothy 4:7, 8, 12, 16. Paul shares with Timothy his vision of trust and character.

- What does Paul mean by "train yourself to be godly"?
- Why does Paul place credibility in the same category with godliness?
- What does the word "integrity" mean in this passage?

Taking It Home

Many business leaders believe that ethics must be restored to the marketplace.

- Why is a return to integrity crucial to your business life?
- Mention three ways in which your word is your bond.
- What needs to be strengthened in your character so that you are honest, even when no one is looking?

Chapter 6

If It's Broken, Fix It!

In 1938 the University of Tennessee played the University of Alabama in their annual football game in Knoxville, Tennessee, for the Southeastern Conference championship. My father drove to that football game, along with a load of football players from Portland High School in Middle Tennessee. After the game was over, they were driving home, and just outside of Portland as Dad rounded a curve, a man in another car ran Dad's car off the road. Dad hit a telephone pole so hard that it broke into three pieces. His face went into the steering column, and the players were thrown from the car with many being injured. (This was long before airbags and seat belts.)

When my father hit the steering column, his face was torn and shattered. My mother held his blood-drenched face over a dishpan in the ambulance all the way to Vanderbilt University Hospital. Dad went through a great deal of surgery over the next several months and spent months and years working to be sure that his teeth were useable, but slowly his body began to heal. If you have been in a serious car wreck, you can identify with my dad's experience, particularly when your body is broken and you begin to see the repair that takes place.

Dr. Paul Brand, in his excellent book *Fearfully and Wonderfully Made*, tells the story of a medical team working on assignment in India. He recalls an engineer coming into his clinic with a serious problem. The man's neck twitched so violently and uncontrollably that his chin would smash into his right shoulder. Dr. Brand, a very fine surgeon, operated on him by going into the base of the brain and working with the nerves in such a way that he was finally able to correct this man's problem.

On a less dramatic level, you may have had a bad cold, the flu, or some other problem in your body. Bacteria can enter your body in one way or another, and as a result the body's immune system goes to work and fights for your health. Without your immune system, you die.

If we compare the spiritual Body, the church, to the human body, as Paul did, we can begin to understand how our spiritual immune system works. How do you build a strong immune system in the Body of Jesus Christ? What are the common dysfunctions and problems that occur in the church? How do we prevent division, heartache, and other problems in the Body from overcoming it so that it becomes unhealthy?

When bacteria enters your physical body, white blood cells immediately rush to the damaged site and begin to rebuild it. A small drop of blood contains about seven thousand white cells. Every one of those white cells is dedicated to preventing bacteria from taking over your body.

You may not see them, but your kidneys are very valuable. One-fourth of the blood from one of your heartbeats runs down your renal artery to your kidneys. The kidneys filter out of the bloodstream about thirty harmful chemicals that are then carried away to the bladder for expulsion.

If you suffer a broken bone, a massive gash, or severe pain, your blood rushes immediately to the afflicted area and begins to fight for your health.

Orthopedic surgeons tell us that when we experience pain in our hip joints, or in our hands, the cartilage is filled with tiny channels that pump fluid to alleviate the pressure. As your joint slowly moves, those fluids precede movement and begin to cushion that area so that you can withstand the pressure and pain. The lubrication system in the human body is astonishing.

What are the common problems, pains, and dysfunctions that inflict the Body of Christ and make it unhealthy so that it begins to die? Following are five major dysfunctions that the Bible says can occur in the church.

Stagnation. You know that in your own body you must have a balance of proper food, exercise, and rest in order to function properly. The same is true for the Body of Christ. We must ingest the Word of God in a healthy way. We have to exercise and rest, or else stagnation will set in and destroy our health. Then the Body of Christ no longer grows.

That was precisely the problem in a church that existed two thousand years ago—the church at Laodicea. She was experiencing stagnation, as John described in his revelation: "To the angel of the church in Laodicea write: These are the words of the Amen, the faithful and true witness, the rule of God's creation. I know your deeds, that you are neither cold nor hot. I wish you were either one or the other! So, because you are lukewarm—neither hot nor cold—I am about to spit you out of my mouth" (Revelation 3:14-16).

Stagnation was killing the church at Laodicea. John said that because they were not eating and exercising properly, they were not growing. They had stagnated.

Self-Centeredness. The purpose of the church is to reach out. But when a church forgets who she is, she reaches *in* and focuses only on herself. When a church turns inward and talks only to herself, she dies.

The Great Physician wants a healthy, active Body, always reaching out to lost people. Why? Because that's who they are meant to be. Jesus was always found among the people, and He calls His church to go where He would go. "Therefore, as we have opportunity, let us do good to all people, especially to those who belong to the family of believers" (Galatians 6:10).

The early church followed His example well: "All the believers were together and had everything in common. Selling their possessions and goods, they gave to anyone as he had need. Every day they continued to meet together in the temple courts. They broke bread in their homes and ate together with glad and sincere hearts, praising God and enjoying the favor of all the people. And the Lord added to their number daily those who were being saved" (Acts 2:44-47).

Why did the church "have favor with all the people"? Because they were out among the people. They fed and clothed them, showed love to them, and shared with them the story of Jesus Christ. Jesus described His church as light, salt, and leaven. What is the similarity among these figures of speech? All are about affecting the world. The idea of the church is never to turn inward—it is always to focus outward, as Mark noted: "Go into all the world and preach the good news to all creation. Whoever believes and is baptized will be saved" (Mark 16:15, 16). And Hebrews encourages us this way: "Let us, then, go to him outside the camp, bearing the disgrace he bore" (Hebrews 13:13).

Bound to Traditions. When faith becomes routine and worship becomes ritual, religion becomes tradition. When people challenge us for the reason for our faith and all we can say is, "That's the way we've always done it," then the Body begins to die. The chains of tradition prevent life and growth. And we hear the rattle of death approaching when we cease to know why we believe what we believe and act on it.

I was only eighteen and a new freshman in college at David Lipscomb University when Willard Collins asked his morning Bible class this question: "Why is it that we in churches of Christ use a cappella music?"

This was one of those times when I thought everyone in the room knew the answer. No hands went up, but I was convinced that most of the students in the room knew the answer and thought he had asked a rhetorical question. We sing because *we* are the instruments: "Sing and make melody in your heart to the Lord" (Ephesians 5:19b), we are told in the New Testament. The early church sang, worshiped, and praised God (Colossians 3:16).

A young lady on the back row of our class finally raised her hand and said, "We just do." In her mind, the reason we sing in worship was because that's our unique tradition, and we had always done it. It had nothing to do with worship or with each Christian being an instrument of music in praise of God.

Unless a church understands the reason for its faith and practice, it is vulnerable to tradition. Jesus says this is a real problem because of what it can mean in your life: "You nullify the word of God for the sake of your traditions" (Matthew 15:6). Paul then wrote to a church that he wanted to be healthy: "See to it that no one takes you captive through hollow and deceptive philosophy, which depends on human tradition and the basic principles of this world rather than on Christ" (Colossians 2:8).

Why must the focus exclusively be on Christ and not on human tradition? Maybe the answer is found in understanding our own human body. You and I are five minutes from death. If we are deprived of air, we turn blue, first around our toes and fingernails, then our lips, tongue, and extremities. Physicians tell us these are outward signs of an internal struggle. Only Christ offers His Body the Holy Spirit, the Body's breath. No wonder David cried, "So my soul pants for you, O God" (Psalm 42:1). Only the Spirit of God, not human traditions, dramatically lives in the Body of Christ and gives it eternal life. Understandably Paul warns, "Do not grieve the Holy Spirit of God with whom you were sealed for the day of redemption" (Ephesians 4:30). To be a healthy Body, God's Spirit makes the church more loving, holy, and God-like.

Non-Compliance. When a church *selectively* obeys God, it quickly becomes sick. Do we comply with all of the Word of God? Do we refuse to follow some of the teaching of God because it is uncomfortable, or it doesn't push our buttons? Do we fail to comply because we don't understand why God is asking us to obey?

Confusion centers around the issue of obedience. Obedience is not legalism but the natural response of a surrendered heart to the will of God. It is complying with God's Word, whether we understand His reason for our compliance or not. Obedience is an index of how much we love God. So Jesus claims, "If you love me, you will do what I command" (John 14:15). And He said, "Whoever has my commands and obeys them, he is the one who loves me" (John 14:21). Submission to God's will is not salvation by works, but a compliant, grateful heart responding to God. "This is love for God: to obey his commands. And his commands are not burdensome, for every one born of God has overcome the world. This is the victory that has overcome the world, even our faith" (1 John 5:3, 4).

So God is greatly concerned when He sees a church suffering from non-compliance: "To the angel of the church in Sardis write: These are the words of him who holds the seven spirits of God and the seven stars. I know your deeds: you have a reputation of being alive, but you are dead. Wake up! Strengthen what remains and is about to die, for I have not found your deeds complete in the sight of my God. Remember, therefore, what you have received and heard; obey it, and repent. But if you do not wake up, I will come like a thief, and you will not know at what time I will come to you" (Revelation 3:1).

Their problem is not that they don't know the Word of God, but they won't obey it. You have a reputation, but you are really dying because you are suffering from the dysfunction of non-compliance. You're not obeying the Word of God as it has been taught to you.

Driven by Culture. Shall a church be driven by its own calling or by circumstances outside itself? Shall a church define its mission, worship, and work by who it is intended to be or by the culture around it?

The church has largely been uncritical of three revolutions which have deeply impacted our culture. In the 1950s, following World War II, our culture experienced a *prosperity revolution*. Women went to work in record numbers, and the American dream became to own one's home. Families had two sources of income, more money than ever before. Dollar marks spelled success, and we had more to live with than ever before. Our grandparents would have been shocked at our standard of living. Many Christians began to earn large amounts of money. At this point the church should have been more careful, more critical of a culture bent on prosperity. Such a culture did not nurture relationships but valued money and tempted us to gradually become a part of it. And we did!

In the 1960s an *ethical revolution* overwhelmed our culture. Absolute truth took a backseat to relativism. Situation ethics replaced the Ten Commandments. "Johnny no longer knew right from wrong." Neither did Johnny's parents. Perhaps no place in the nation served as a better vantage point for viewing this revolution than the University of California. From 1963-1971 I served on its faculty and daily worked on one of its major campuses in Los Angeles. The University became the epicenter of activity symbolic of a major ethical transition. The Free-Speech Movement, The Jesus Movement, the bombing of the Bank of America, daily class discussions about values, the antiwar movement—these were just a few of the expressions of an ethical revolution that would affect our entire culture. Instead of being alarmed at a total shift of values, many Christians simply expressed dismay at long hair. The church seemed to be more concerned with how young people looked than what they believed and did. Today these young people are baby boomers.

Also in the 1960s, a *therapeutic revolution* made deep inroads into our understanding of people. Prior to the Sixties, our culture spoke of personal accountability, guilt, and what it meant to be a person. But new views of human nature began to eliminate our previous understanding of guilt, personal responsibility, and accountability. Humanistic understanding replaced divine insight. *I'm Okay, You're Okay* was not only a book title, but it became a life slogan. People were no longer guilty. After everyone was pronounced "okay," our culture wondered why suicide skyrocketed and young people turned in increasing numbers to drugs, and families disintegrated at record rates. While some Christians took note of the therapeutic revolution, many in the church remained uncritical of the revolution. The church, again, had been driven by culture.

Some of Paul's last words when he was about to be executed in Rome were these: "Demas, because he loved this world, has deserted me and has gone to Thessalonica" (2 Timothy 4:10). Earlier Paul had talked about the faith, discipleship, and commitment of Demas, but Demas had been driven by the Roman culture and had been uncritical of it. "Do not love the world or anything in the world. If anyone loves the world, the love of the Father is not in him. For everything in the world—the cravings of sinful man, the lust of his eyes and the boasting of what he has and does—comes not from the Father but from the world. The world and its desires pass away, but the man who does the will of God lives forever" (1 John 15).

Over and over our culture is at odds with God. He fosters relationships, but the culture fosters individualism, materialism, and even hedonism. Do things to please yourself. Make as much money as you can for your own pleasure. Our entertainment industry is clearly at odds with anything that is wholesome and pure. We are the first generation of Americans to rate our movies based on nudity, language, and violence. Why? If you have been to a movie lately, you probably saw a lot of people killed violently, or heard God's name used in obscenities, or both. God says don't fall in love with the world and its possessions. Our culture fosters a disconnected lifestyle.

God wants us to be a part of a healthy Body that has a strong immune system. The Bible presents at least five different ways to build up such an immune system.

Close Fellowship. By building strong relationships in an atmosphere of loving concern, we can build up the immune system to stand against attack, bacteria, and all kinds of infection that threaten the Body of Christ. A small-group atmosphere is a wonderful way of nurturing and getting to know one another, and sharing together. Close fellowship builds love and concern in a congregation. The simple activities of praying together, talking together, eating together, playing together, and working together build relationships. Strong relationships represent a strong immune system.

Deeper Discipleship. After our conversion to Jesus, we spend the rest of our lives learning to follow Him. Some have been taught to follow the church, but the Bible does not say "follow my church." What Jesus said was *"follow me."* By following the church we follow each other. But when we follow Jesus Christ we will get closer to Him, walk in His sandals, and come to know Him. A church that deepens its discipleship of Jesus by following Him is building an immune system.

Celebrative Worship. Worship is praising God for *who He is*. It is acknowledging Jesus Christ as Lord and Savior, celebrating His death, burial, and resurrection. Worship is seeking God, not just seeking an *experience* with God. Some churches define worship as having an experience with God, but this makes the worshiper the judge, arbiter, and critic of whether or not he had a worship experience. Some leave the worship service saying, "Well, I didn't get much out of worship today. I didn't know those songs. I didn't understand the preacher's message. I didn't have much of an experience with God."

What if worship were not designed to provide you with an experience with God, but designed to have you seek God? Suppose God is the audience. What would happen if we were totally fatigued after a worship service of seeking, praising, and adoring God? Yet when you seek God, He lifts your soul and spirit. He causes you to be so close to Him that you can't describe it with words.

Isaiah said, "Holy, holy, holy . . . Woe to me! I am ruined. For I am a man of unclean lips, and my eyes have seen the King, the Lord Almighty" (Isaiah 6:3, 5).

Isaiah said that! If Isaiah needed to repent, I'm sure I do, too. So the first thing a worshiper should do is pray and repent of his sins and seek God. Paul said when we seek that relationship with God, "He is not far from us." We can worship Him in spirit and in truth. Celebrative worship seeks God and builds a healthy Body.

Constant Prayer. When we mobilize prayer, we stay healthy. When elders lead us in prayer, pray for us, and pray with us, we become healthy. Paul instructed us to "pray without ceasing" (1 Thessalonians 5:17). Every letter in the New Testament says that a church should pray. Why? Prayer is the only power that affects God, affects others, and affects us. I must confess that on a few occasions in my life I have even been frightened by the power of prayer. Prayer brings me so close to the power and mystery of God's providence. It is awesome! Indescribable! Unbelievable! A church on its knees builds its immune system against the attacks of Satan.

Broader Evangelism. You never judge an army's strength by how many people sit in the mess hall. An army is judged by how many people are on the front lines fighting the war. A healthy church shares its faith in Christ with others. We sometimes think we cannot do that unless we go through a long, long list of doctrines concerning the church. But what people really want to know is:

- Who is Jesus to you?
- What was your life like before He became your Lord and Savior?
- How did you become a Christian?
- Is Christianity making any difference in your life?

People want to know who God is to you and if the relationship with God is making a difference in your life.

There are many differences between a healthy and an unhealthy church. When a church emphasizes one purpose to the neglect of all others, it becomes unbalanced and unhealthy, stunted and dysfunctional, asleep and vulnerable to disease. A healthy church has a strong immune system. It's working, balanced, and quick to deal with invasive bacteria so that it may stay strong and healthy.

Not long ago, I was talking with a good friend who had served in the administration of Pepperdine University. We were talking about some of the current problems facing the church today. He paused in our conversation, then drew my attention to a characteristic in the church often overlooked: "The church is extremely resilient. She has survived martyrdom, accusations, misunderstandings, and self-righteousness, and yet she lives on today."

What accounts for such resiliency? How do we bring healing and resiliency to the Body of Christ? Consider these five practical suggestions.

- Listen for the pain in the Body.
- Locate the level of pain in the Body.
- Be gentle with the Body.
- Use God's Word and the Holy Spirit to cure the Body.
- Never give up on the Body.

No wonder God uses the word "body" to describe His church more than any other picture. He knows each part performs a unique function. He reminds us that no part carries on all the functions of the body. He points out that parts of the body depend on each other. Just as your physical body needs regular health check-ups, so must the Body of Christ. We've all known of people who have ignored their doctor's counsel after a health check-up and who have died.

A healthy church never ignores the Great Physician's counsel. After all, it is the Body of Christ and deserves our best attention and commitment.

Thinking It Through

Opening Your Heart

Healing a disease in your body is really the job of the immune system. It prevents and cures diseases through various specialized cells.

- What is the equivalent in a church to the various cells in your body as agents for healing, helping, and showing mercy?
- What is the immune system in a church?

Digging Into God's Word

Turn to 1 Corinthians 12:14-31 where Paul wrote his longest comparison between the church and the human body. Read all three paragraphs he wrote on this topic.

- Why do you suppose a healthy body is united even though composed of a variety of members performing quite different roles?
- Why is a diseased body not at peace?
- Who is the source of peace in a healthy body?
- What have you learned from these insights?

Taking It Home

- What plan of action might be wise for you to take to build up your church?
- Pray for your individual plan of action and include your own family and congregation.

Chapter 7
A Cross, A Yoke, A Towel

A wise old Indian chief once wished to give his property to one of his three sons. He wanted to choose the son who would show the most prowess and promise, so he came up with a test. He took his sons to the foot of a particular mountain and asked each of them to bring back an object to show how far up the mountain he had climbed.

The first son came back with a wildflower in his hand and presented it to his father. The father knew that this wildflower grew only above the timberline, which meant that the son made it more than three-quarters of the way to the top. The second son returned with a red flint stone, which meant that he had been almost to the top of the mountain. The third son returned with nothing. He said, "Father, where I went there was nothing to bring back, but I stood at the summit and looked at the valley below where two great rivers join the ocean." The proud father said, "It has been the ambition of my life that one of my sons would see what you have seen. You have nothing in your hand, but you have a greater thing—you have a vision in your soul."

Vision Is A Necessity

"Where there is no vision the people perish" (Proverbs 29:18). Vision is not an option; it's not something we choose or don't choose. In order to remain faithful to our commitments, we *must* have long-range vision. We must begin to see reality in a different way from those who claim no relation to God.

But what kind of way? What kind of vision? Such vision is much more than what the corporate world calls "strategic planning." And it's certainly more than the process of setting goals for the future. C. S. Lewis said that what Christ really wants in this world are "little Christs"—people with a different set of eyes, eyes that see life as Jesus saw it, people who have spiritual vision.

In 1961, Gwen Hensley and a few others traveled extensively in Russia and the countries of Eastern Europe. The Cold War was in progress, but they began to look at Eastern Europe through different eyes. They saw the possibility of taking Bibles to Russia, Hungary, Poland, Croatia, and other eastern satellite nations. They envisioned families and children reading the Bible in their own language and Christians coming together to form churches in villages and cities. Because it was totally forbidden by law, shipping Bibles into Eastern Europe seemed like a first-class pipe dream. After all, the Iron Curtain had been tightly drawn since 1945. As one young Russian told me: "You have to remember that the wall not only kept you all out, it kept us in."

To practical folks interested in instant success, the notion of printing Bibles in the various Eastern European languages and getting them through the Iron Curtain seemed laughable. How would you raise money for such a far-fetched dream? How would you translate the money into newly published Bibles? How would you transport them into countries where the reading of the Bible is forbidden by law? These were seemingly insurmountable hurdles, and there was not just one, but many.

But visionaries look beyond what meets the eye. They see further into the future, into possibilities, open doors, and ways of accomplishing goals. Of course, a farmer never looks at a handful of seed and says, "It's just seed." Rather, he sees a field full of grain, loaves in the store, and sliced bread on the table. When parents look down into a crib, they don't say, "Well, another ordinary baby has been born into the world." Instead, they see a physician, an executive, a teacher, or a spiritual leader. Vision sees beyond what meets the physical eye.

By January 1, 1978, Gwen visualized a great ministry of Bible distribution and the Bammel Road church of Houston, Texas, assumed responsibility for Gwen and his wife, Gayle. They chose the name of Eastern European Missions (EEM). In 1982 they decided on Vienna as a base of operations, where they built a publishing house so Austrian printers could produce Bibles of high quality.

Hensley and others began to raise funds to translate the Bible into various Eastern European languages. Soon Bibles in Russian and other languages rolled off the presses. Carefully and privately, Bibles slowly began to be smuggled into Eastern Europe. In 1985, Gwen Hensley died of cancer, but the dream continued.

Two years earlier, Dr. John Sudbury joined EEM to oversee the printing and distribution of Bibles from Vienna. Once while driving in Texas, Sudbury was pulled over by the Texas Highway Patrol. When the officer asked Sudbury his occupation, he responded, "I smuggle Bibles into Russia." The surprised officer quickly gave Sudbury back his driver's license and said, "My wife would kill me if I gave a guy like you a ticket. Just slow down."

At last the Berlin Wall came down in the winter of 1989. Now there was no reason to smuggle Bibles, because Bibles became a treasured commodity. For instance, the longest lines of Russians to visit Moscow's Fair were those who wanted to see a copy of the Bible. By 1991 Russia gave permission for fifty thousand Russian Bibles to come into Moscow, but an ad in a Russian magazine brought two hundred thousand requests for Bibles. Distribution points were set up in cities like Moscow and Rostov-on-Don. Today more than seven million Bibles have been given away in Eastern Europe. Public lectures on the Bible's contents, origin, and style have been well attended by Russians and others. Hundreds of people have read the Bible in their own languages, obeyed its teachings, and formed self-governing churches throughout Eastern Europe. All this happened because of visionaries who saw the world as God sees it and who stayed committed to their vision.

God Sees Us Through the Cross

A Vietnam veteran, finally back in the United States, called his parents from San Francisco. "Dad and Mom, I'm coming home, but I have a special favor to ask. I have a friend I'd like to bring home with me."

"Sure," they said, "we'd like to meet him."

"But there's something you ought to know," the son continued his request. "He was hurt badly in combat. He stepped on a land mine and lost an arm and a leg. He has no home to go to, and I want him to live with us."

"We're so sorry to hear that, son. Maybe we can help him find somewhere to live."

"No, Mom and Dad, I really want him to live with us."

"Son," began the father, "you don't really know what you're asking. A person with such a severe handicap would be a terrible burden on us. We have our own lives to live, and we can't be tied down to someone like that who will constantly interfere with our lives. We think you should come on home and forget about that guy. He'll find some way to live on his own."

At that point, the son hung up the phone, and they never heard from him again. Not long afterwards, the San Francisco police called them. Their son had committed suicide by jumping off a building. The grief-stricken parents flew to California and were taken to the city morgue to identify their son's body. They recognized him, but to their horror, they also discovered something they didn't know. He had only one arm and one leg.

It is easy to love and accept those who are attractive or have great personalities, but the unlovable make us uncomfortable. They're inconvenient, and they interfere with our lives and plans. The irony is that you and I interfere with God's plans, because we are unlovable and inconvenient. But God reaches down into His deepest heart and welcomes us into His family, regardless of how messed up we are. He can do this because of the way He sees us—through the cross.

"But now in Christ Jesus you who once were far away have been brought near through the blood of Christ . . . His purpose was to create in himself one new man out of the two, thus making peace, and in this one body to reconcile both of them to God through the cross, by which he put to death their hostility. He came and preached peace to those who were far away and peace to those who were near" (Ephesians 2:13, 15-17). Not because of anything lovable in us, not because of any really good things we've done, not because of who we are, but because of who He is, He looks at everyone through the cross.

"For God was pleased to have his fullness dwell in him, and through him to reconcile to himself all things, whether things on earth or things in heaven, by making peace through his blood, shed on the cross" (Colossians 1:19, 20). So Peter candidly, boldly tells us "For Christ died for sins once for all, the righteous for the unrighteous, to bring you to God" (1 Peter 3:18). When God looks at you, He sees you through the blood of Jesus.

The cross is primary, central to your salvation and to your forgiveness of all that you've done to interfere with and inconvenience God. That's why we worship, sing our praises to God, enjoy His Spirit, relax in His promises, and urge others to accept Him. But an increasing number of us seem not to be convinced. We bow down before the "god of tolerance" in an effort to be as broadminded as possible. We begin to reason, "Maybe Mohammed or Buddha do provide ways to God and eternal life. Maybe God will accept us regardless." Yet, salvation is found only in Jesus Christ for one primary reason—He died on the cross for you and me! He gave His blood on the cross to bring us to God. "I am the way," said Jesus, "the truth and the life, and no man comes to the Father but through me." Neither Mohammed nor Buddha died on the cross for your guilt.

God only sees us through the cross—the cross stained with the cleansing blood of His precious Son. He'll meet you at the foot of the cross, but nowhere else, for that's where He is!

We See Each Other Through a Yoke

What's a yoke? It's neither a word nor a thing with which you may be familiar. A yoke is a double wooden collar placed over the necks of two oxen to hold them together as a team so they can work together in harmony and help each other pull their load. Such a scene was quite familiar to Jesus and is still common in some countries today. So Jesus uses the word "yoke" in a fascinating way to symbolize our relationship with Him and with each other: "Come to me, all you who are weary and burdened, and I will give you rest. Take my yoke upon you and learn from me, for I am gentle and humble in heart, and you will find rest for your souls. For my yoke is easy and my burden is light" (Matthew 11:28-30). What an interesting symbol of relationships!

What do you think is Jesus' leading characteristic? How do most people know Him? Even unbelievers recognize His limitless unconditional love for people. "God is love," wrote John. Jesus spent His ministry in loving people. His love knew no restrictions; so He touched the untouchables, reached out to the blind, the homeless, the nameless, women and children, the forgotten and lonely. He went into homes to eat with the despised and sinful people of the land. He partied with the irreligious and the secular. He spent time also with the affluent, the well-known, and the educated. In the end, He died on a cross for all of them, but only for one reason—because He loved people more than they loved themselves. He saw each one as valuable and of great worth, not for the normal reasons of money, power, and fame, but because God created each to be like Him.

So Christ places His neck in one side of the yoke and calls on you to place your neck in the other side. Let Him lead. Learn from Him. Do what He does. Behave toward others the way He behaved toward them. Walk where He walks, and go where He takes you. He wants us to be His yoke-people.

Community—the Vision of God

Before the foundation of the world, the Father, Son, and Holy Spirit lived in a perfect community. In the Trinity, there was communication, love, mutual respect, and a sense of belonging. Even the first words of the Bible suggest plurality: "In the beginning, God (plural) created the heavens and the earth" (Genesis 1:1). So when God completed His creative activity by bringing mankind into being, He said, "Let *us* make man in our own image" (Genesis 1:27).

God as community envisions a community like the Trinity, a group of people that will reflect the likeness of the Godhead. In the New Testament people didn't call this group *Christian* first at Antioch, but *Christians* (plural). God didn't make us to live the Christian life alone, but in community with others.

John Donne, in *Devotions*, wrote, "No man is an island, entire of itself; every man is a piece of the continent, a part of the main." Donne simply recognized that people are made for relationships. It's the way we are created. God calls the church to image the Trinity in our relationships with each other. We are to behave toward one another as the Father, Son, and Holy Spirit behave toward each other—in unity, harmony, cooperation, and communion. You see, God knows that the world will be impressed when it sees a group of people yoked together, loving each other, and serving each other.

Our world hungers for true community. Many songs, books, movies, and TV shows are about community and a person's need for relationships. Several years ago, the University of Louisville Medical School conducted research on cadavers of those who had lived lonely, friendless lives and on those who had lived friendly, intimate lives. Their conclusion was startling: The brain cells of the lonely had shrunk, hardened, and died. Meanwhile, those who lived lives of strong relationships had brain cells that were vibrant, active, and well-nourished. In an alienated world where people are treated like numbers, God envisions a community where people are not property, but persons of ultimate value and worth.

People won't find intimacy in government, in the workplace, or in education. Unfortunately, they may not find it in the church community either. In a message to a Dallas congregation, one of its most esteemed leaders said, "As we have sought to restore early Christianity, I think we got church organization right. I think we got baptism right. I think we got the Lord's Supper right. But we didn't get relationships right!"

Division, confusion, gossip, and debate have marked too many churches instead of peace, love, and intimacy. We've not learned how to show mutual respect to one another when we disagree. We've confused approval with acceptance, failing to see that Christ approved of almost no one, but accepted everyone. For example, He accepted the woman caught in the act of adultery and did not condemn her though she deserved it. But He certainly disapproved of her sex life and told her in no uncertain terms to stop it. We've even shot our wounded when they really needed us. Some churches have not yet learned to be a community. "We didn't get relationships right!"

Yet, God still envisions a community that people long for and want. He wants us to look at one another through a yoke, to work in harmony, cooperation, and mutual respect. Ask yourself these questions:

- Do the unchurched see us exhibiting loving acceptance of each other?
- Do the unchurched sense a family spirit in us?
- Do they see us pull each other's loads?
- Do they perceive joy and commitment in our community?

As the church, we're on the right track when we have the eyes of God and look at each other, not in judgment, not in condemnation, not focusing on weaknesses, but accepting, loving, and caring for one another. "So by this shall all men know that you are my disciples, that you love one another" (John 13:35).

Try to be more loving toward your fellow Christians. It's not easy, but the cross was no picnic either! If you think it's easy to turn the other cheek, try it. When we're loving each other as yoke people, we're living the gospel of Christ as God dreamed it.

We See the Unchurched Through a Towel

John describes a remarkable moment just before Jesus went to Gethsemane to die: "Jesus knew that the Father had put all things under his power, and that he had come from God and was returning to God; so he got up from the meal, took off his outer clothing, and wrapped a towel around his waist. After that, he poured water into a basin and began to wash his disciples' feet, drying them with the towel that was wrapped around him" (John 13:3-5).

When he had finished washing their feet, Jesus asked them if they understood what He had done for them. Then He told them to go do as He had done. The towel represents the untiring service of Jesus to the world. In this extraordinary moment we see a symbol of that service: a towel. Jesus went from apostle to apostle, removing their dirty sandals, washing their feet in a basin of water, then drying their feet with a towel—a picture of selfless service to the world. He has given us the dignity of His work—service to others. He is no longer here to wash feet and carry burdens, but He has left His church to look at the unchurched world through a towel. Our work is washing feet, bearing burdens, and serving others.

George Barna's book *Index of Leading Spiritual Indicators* rated the Salvation Army as the church group most favored in America by Americans. What I know about the Salvation Army is that every December, around Christmas, they ring bells and collect money to use in assisting poor and needy people. During a crisis, usually the first people to come with food and aid is the Salvation Army. Isn't it interesting that people in America, who do not attend any church, say the one religious group that impresses them most is the group that feeds, helps, and cares for people?

Committed followers of Jesus Christ see the world through a towel of service. God dreams of a community of people who are generous, positive, and constantly serving others. On the Day of Judgment we're not going to be asked how many church services we attended, although that's important to our spiritual growth. The questions will be, "How many hospitals did you visit? How many hungry people did you feed? How many homeless children did you shelter? How many prisons did you visit? How much hospitality did you show to strangers? How many grieving people did you comfort? How many souls did you touch with the Word?"

The challenge of our lives today is the challenge of serving people. In a world that has lost its vision and direction, God wants us to be committed to *His* vision of serving people and taking care of their needs. If we do that, we won't have to worry about converting the world. The world will naturally follow us to Christ, the One whose love they see through our service.

God sees us through the cross. We should see each other through His yoke. And we should see the unchurched world through His towel. God looks at His world and doesn't dream an impossible dream; He dreams a possible dream—a dream of Christian people committed to His vision and living out that commitment in their daily lives as servants of the cross yoked together in love.

*"Some men see things as they are and say, 'Why?'
I dream things that never were and say, 'Why not?'"*

—George Bernard Shaw

Thinking It Through

Opening Your Heart

Jesus knew what a cross, a yoke, and a towel were like in His world. What are some equivalents for a cross, a yoke, and a towel today?

- What stands for sacrifice, community, and ministry in today's world?
- How would you describe the meaning of sacrifice, community, and ministry?

Digging Into God's Word

After Jesus predicted His death in Matthew 16:21, He shared His vision for His disciples in Matthew 16:22-28.

- Read these seven verses (21-28).
- Why does Jesus place the cross ahead of following Him as a disciple?
- Should community come before or after ministry? Why?

Taking It Home

If you are personally to renew your commitment to
God's dream, several practical questions will help you
do that.

- What do you need to pray for as you renew your commitment to God's dream?
- What will be your goal this month in making God's vision for your life a reality?
- Where do you sense God leading you to begin your renewal to commitment? At home? At work? Somewhere else?

Chapter 8
Jesus Never Ran

The city of Detroit was in shock. Deletha Word—age 33, height 5' 1", weight 133 pounds—was grabbed by a man as she was getting into her car and severely beaten. She broke away from him and started running across a Detroit bridge. Martel Welch—age 20, height 6' 4", weight 260 pounds—chased her along the bridge with a tire iron in his hand. Fearful for her life, Deletha jumped off the bridge . . . to her death.

The city of Detroit was, rightfully, appalled by the incident. Welch was found guilty and given a harsh sentence. Equally shocking to the people of Detroit was that forty people witnessed the attack and did not come to her aid as Deletha Ward screamed for help.

To not respond to people's screams, to not show compassion when they are in pain, to not serve people in the world, are not options for people who are committed to Jesus Christ. Even people who are not active church members know that Jesus reaches out to help everyone, regardless of who they are, and so should His followers.

First Base

The late Henri J. M. Nouwen, author of numerous works dealing with our contemporary search for spirituality, insightfully gives us the three disciplines of the Son of God. Nouwen's understanding of these disciplines helps to form the foundation for this chapter. He suggests the spiritual order in the life of Jesus is that He first went to the mountain alone to pray: "One of those days Jesus went into the hills to pray, and spent the night praying to God" (Luke 6:12). He engaged in solitude. He went to first base. Solitude is more than privacy. It's in solitude with God that you can meet yourself, God, and Christ. You're alone, but not lonely. Why is it so important that you be alone with God? Perhaps, it's because solitude is where you can listen to the voice of the One who loves you and who can speak to the very heart of your being.

- Moses spent forty years in the city, but he didn't meet God until he went to the desert. In solitude God broke his pride and prepared his heart for great leadership.
- Elijah fled south to the desert after his greatest victory as a prophet. In solitude God refreshed him in a "still small voice."
- David ran from King Saul and lived in the desert. In solitude, he penned many of his psalms that focus on worship and meditation.
- Paul, having just been baptized, spent three years in the Arabian desert. In solitude, he met God who began to strengthen him for his new ministry.

So, too, Jesus met God in solitude, where His vision was clarified, His mind was cleared, and His spirit was strengthened by focusing on His Father. It's also in solitude where your sins are forgiven and where you receive strength and power. No wonder Jesus went to the desert so often. It's not just a piece of parched ground; it's not even a place. Solitude involves withdrawal, aloneness, quietness with God, and it's where promises are made or renewed.

Second Base

Then Jesus went on to second base. According to Luke 6:13, "When morning came, he called his disciples to him, and chose twelve of them, whom he also designated apostles." So after he went to the mountain top to pray, Nouwen says Jesus gathered around Him a community of people called apostles. He built relationships and networks with these men. He ate with them, listened to them, taught them. He forgave them and communicated intimately with them.

It's remarkable to me that solitude always seems to call us to people, to community, and the order seems to be important. In other words, solitude comes before community because love, understanding, worship, forgiveness, and celebration make a community. So Jesus teaches us how important relationships are and that we are not Christians alone. Joy and fellowship come through commitment to spiritual community.

Third Base

According to Nouwen, having experienced the solitude of God and the community of men, Jesus moved on to ministry: "He went down with them and stood on a level place. A large crowd of his disciples were there and a great number of people from all over Judea, from Jerusalem, and from the seacoast of Tyre and Sidon, who had come to hear him and to be healed of their diseases" (Luke 6:17). Notice the order. Jesus didn't start with ministry. That would be like running to third base first. He started with commitment to God, developed a community of support, then began to serve. Each of these is not something you *do*, but something you *are*. You must allow God room in your own spiritual life to act. That's why you go to first base before you go to second, then third.

How shall we understand commitment to ministry? Its meaning becomes clear through a marvelous story—the story of Jesus.

The Story of Jesus (Matthew 17)

Four people slowly made their way up the mountainside. They lived outdoors mainly, and they were tired. When they reached a level place, and as twilight began to settle over them, they wanted to sleep. Three of them did sleep—Peter, James, and John. But the carpenter from Nazareth, unable to sleep, sat alone with His troubling thoughts.

A week earlier He had said to these men and to the other apostles in His community that He would have to die on a cross. He was speaking of dying, but they kept thinking about living. He said, "If you're going to follow me, you must deny yourselves and take up your cross."

He spoke of self-denial, but they were still thinking about victory over the Roman government. They had yet to turn to the right frequency. They nodded their heads every time He spoke, and they thought they understood, but they didn't. For Jesus it was like preaching sermons or singing to the deaf. How was He to go on? They seemed to think that He wanted to run the Romans out of the country and establish a new political and social kingdom like in the days of David, but He had nothing like that in mind. Jesus was not interested in ruling the Romans, but He was interested in ruling the hearts of the apostles, and they didn't understand.

Frustrated and discouraged, our Lord did the only thing He could do. He closed His eyes and prayed to God. When the Father saw and heard Him, it must have broken His great heart. The Father, the Holy Spirit, and Jesus had decided eons earlier that the Son would come to earth, that He would gather some dedicated men around Him, and that He would train those men to carry on the spiritual work of His life. But they didn't understand; they just didn't get it. They weren't even sure who He was. One day they argued with each other, and the next day they promised to obey Him. In one moment out of one mouth came, "You're the Son of God." In the next moment, out of another mouth came arguments over who would sit on his right and left. Each time the loving heart of God broke again.

Then one of the most spectacular events in all of history happened. "As he was praying the appearance of his face changed, and his clothes became as bright as a flash of lightning" (Luke 9:29). For one brief moment God lifted the humanity of Jesus and gave Him back His eternity. He was transfigured. That is, He became as He had been before He came to this world and put on a human body. He was in His glory as the eternal God, the Son. A radiance shone forth from Him—a brilliance that flashed like lightning. God reminded Him that He would soon be home again as glorious ruler of the universe.

On one side of Jesus stood Moses, the lawgiver. Only God knew where Moses had died and had been buried. On the other side of him stood Elijah, the great prophet. Elijah didn't die but was translated from earth to heaven. The three spiritual giants talked about Jesus' departure from the earth and His coming home to be with them in heaven. They doubtless reminded Jesus that death was meaningless. Perhaps they said, "You are going to die, Jesus, but death has no power over you. Your work will go on. Heaven is near, and you are God the Son. You will reign forever and ever as Lord of lords and King of kings."

The cloud quickly began to cover all three of them, and from the heart of the cloud an eternal voice said, "This is my son, whom I love. With him I am well pleased; listen to him" (Luke 9:34, 35). What Jesus needed was reaffirmation from God, the Father. Frustrated and depressed over the apostles' lack of understanding, He needed to hear the Father speak with clarity. Peter, James, and John needed to hear it too.

For Peter, James, and John the scene was unbelievable. How could they ever tell anybody about this? Face to face with God! They had heard the voice of the Father as he affirmed who Jesus was in their very presence. "This is my beloved Son." This was not Moses the lawgiver or Elijah the prophet. This was not just another great man. This was the one and only Son of God. "Listen to him."

To prolong that moment with God, to stay on the mountain top with him, Peter made a suggestion: "Master, it is good for us to be here. Let us put up three shelters—one for you, one for Moses, and one for Elijah" (Luke 9:33). Some suggestions are good ones, but this one wasn't! Peter, not knowing what to say, went ahead and said it. Terrified by the transfiguration, Peter fell with his face to the ground. But notice the response of Jesus: "Get up, don't be afraid."

Matthew and Luke said that Jesus led them down the mountain into the valley below where a large crowd of people met Jesus. Among them was the father of an epileptic, a boy who had been so possessed by evil that he was an embarrassment to his mother and a shame to the family name. At any unpredictable moment, especially in public, he began to froth and convulse and scream. The pain of that family was so real. Jesus healed the boy and returned him whole to his family. "And they were all amazed at the greatness of God" (Luke 9:43).

Mountain Top Experience

In the Transfiguration story Jesus is showing us more than we can possibly see or comprehend. This is one of the climactic moments in His ministry and life. Here are two important things He reveals to us:

It is on the mountain top that God is near. When we experience closeness to God, we worship Him with enthusiasm, passion, and joy. We're on top of the mountain experiencing an eternal moment. Worship affirms who Jesus is, and the theme of worship is "This is my beloved Son in whom I am well pleased. Listen to him." Believe in your heart this magnificent theme, and let your spirit bow down in awe and reverence before Jesus. Be committed to Him.

Silently the bread and wine speak in careful, articulate, and eloquent ways. What could be more intimate than eating with Christ? The fellowship of joy is among us as we talk and see and grieve, hug and kiss. The praise is glorious when we sing to our Lord, and the theme of the mountain top is always the same: "This is my beloved Son in whom I am well pleased. Listen to him." It is the affirmation of who Jesus really is. And it singles Him out as the only one worthy to be worshiped and praised.

How easy it is to become confused over what worship is and what it is not. The story of the mountain top clarifies both questions. Jesus is the audience, and we are the players.

Perhaps you go out of town during the week on your job, or maybe you go to work at a corporation and sit at a computer during the week. You may have two little children at home, so you're constantly changing diapers, washing, and ironing, or you're stuck in a traffic jam on a freeway. What do you need? You need to come together with others at least once a week on top of the mountain and have God affirm for your soul once again that "This is my beloved Son, in whom I am well pleased. Listen to him."

Many voices shout at you:

"Work hard."
"Don't just stand there—do something."
"Prove you're worth something."
"What have you done for us recently?"
"You're number one."

As the voices of our culture scream out to us to make bad choices, there is one overwhelming voice on top of the mountain saying, "This is my beloved Son in whom I am well pleased. Listen to him." Hear Him above the confusion and noise in the world. Tune your frequency only to His voice. God affirms every week that Jesus is worthy of your worship. Listen to His voice.

From time to time people ask me, "How do you keep worship from becoming routine?" I don't know how to answer that because, if you're on the mountain top, how can it be routine? This is not entertainment; it's worship! When you come together with other Christians to worship and experience beautiful songs of praise, take the Lord's Supper, and hear the Word of God, how can it be routine? Each time is new because we've never had this particular experience on this particular day on the mountain top. We live in pain, stress, dysfunction, guilt, and sin. We're coming to the mountain top to hear only one thing: "This is my beloved Son, in whom I am well pleased. Listen to him."

Worship is never routine, for it is a joy, a passion, ever exciting and new. Each period of worship is an eternal moment that never has occurred before and will never occur again. It's the experience of the mountain top—a moment of spiritual transformation, the result and the reward of unwavering commitment to Christ and His ministry.

Valley Experience

This same great story also teaches us that *Jesus calls us down to the valley of ministry.* Like Peter, we all want to stay on top of the mountain. Don't you love Peter? He says, "This is so great up here Lord, why don't we just camp out? Why don't we build three shelters—one for you, one for Elijah, and one for Moses—and just stay here? This is fantastic, Lord! Why don't we just stay on top of the mountain?"

Sadly, the disciples of Jesus who stay on top of the mountain have quit following Him, for Jesus has descended to the valley below, Matthew and Luke say. If you stay on top of the mountain, instead of looking at Christ, all you do is look at each other, because He is not there.

A church that only worships will soon find itself looking only at one another. You have the same kind of problem as children do when it snows. After the children have romped and shouted and played in the snow for two or three days, they come in the house and start looking at each other and getting on each others' nerves. "I don't want him so close to me." "She touched me!" "He got on my bed!" They get cabin fever, and soon they are quarreling, scrapping with one another, drawing lines, and putting up "no trespassing" signs.

Some churches do that, too. They try to stay on the mountain top, thinking that's what Christianity is all about, but Jesus is in the valley of ministry. They look only at each other until they quarrel, split, cause discord with one another, and put up "no trespassing" signs. They spend a lot of their time talking to each other in a language that only they understand. The longer they stay on top of the mountain, the more they look at each other, and the more they quarrel and hurt one another.

If we're committed to Jesus, we must follow Him down into the valley, because that's where the epileptics and the dysfunctional families are. That's where the alcoholics and divorced people are. That's where the children live who don't know who their daddies are, where everybody who is playing emotional games and wearing masks live, where you find pain, poverty, and hopelessness. That's where God is—down among the people who need Him.

The valley is where service takes place and where ministry happens. Prisoners, street people, and dirty people are in the valley. People who have given up on life and given up on God are in the valley. Confused students who believe life is all about making money live in the valley. And 25-year-old couples who are starting families, buying large homes and new cars—they're down in the valley, too. They live next door to a man with a hideous disease, a daughter whose mother has just died, a divorcing couple in deep emotional and spiritual pain. The valley is where we see problems and suffering.

Ministry isn't something you *do;* it's something you *allow.* Ministry isn't making a list in your daytimer and saying, "Today I'll do six things to serve people." Ministry is leaving worship to impact city life and our families at home. It's allowing the power that you receive in worship to strengthen you to become a channel of that power to hurting and desperate people. Every time you're around people, you're around sin, pain, guilt, and hurt. They are looking for Christ, and you are His conduit. But the power that comes through you is not anything you learned. It's not a matter of competency, education, or status in life. The power is His; you are only a transmitter.

It reminds me of a radio network. The national head-quarters sends out an important message on a certain frequency. All along the way, radio stations and power boosters in that network recharge that message and send it out again. Eventually, the message is received and rebroadcast on local stations. At last, the message is picked up by individual receivers and broadcast directly into the homes and businesses of people like you and me who need to know the news.

In the same way God sent out His saving message of grace through prophets and priests and kings. Jesus recharged the message and sent it out again from the cross. Christians around the world continue to receive the message and rebroadcast it locally. At last, through people like you and me the saving message reaches people directly in their homes and businesses down here in the valley. The effectiveness of the network depends on how well we have our receivers tuned into God's frequency. Are we power boosters for His message of grace?

I think that's why at times you see brand new Christians who have the immense power of God in them, and you see other people that became Christians fifty or sixty years ago who are not doing anything.

Other times you see an 85-year-old who is vital and powerful, while a young teenager with all the enthusiasm of their teen years is dull and apathetic. In each case the power of God is either being allowed or shut off. It doesn't matter who you are, which school you attended, or where you live. What matters is that you are in the valley with people, and you are allowing the power of God to work through your life right at that moment. That's why Luke and Matthew say that Jesus went down to the valley because ministry thrives there.

Do you know a lot of people outside your church circle? When that question is asked of most preachers, they respond that most of their work is with members of their churches, and they know very few people who are not members of their churches. In his excellent little book *Working the Angles,* Eugene H. Peterson tells us what has happened to so many preachers and their churches: They "have metamorphosed into a company of shopkeepers, and the shops they keep are churches. They are preoccupied with shopkeepers' concerns—how to keep the customers happy, how to lure customers away from competitors down the street, how to package the goods so that the customers will lay out more money." Sadly, they are not down in the valley with Jesus.

Be compassionate with people in the valley. They likely don't know much about the Bible or the Restoration Movement. They probably don't know how to find Isaiah in the Old Testament or Philippians in the New Testament; they may not even own a Bible, at least not one that they know how to use or understand. If they come to one of your worship services, they will probably sit in the back, and they won't want anyone to know their names. They'll rush out quickly because they are uncomfortable being on the mountain top when they've been in the valley for so long. They need patient help in ascending from the valley to the mountain.

For the last twenty years, Barbara and I have made that walk with unchurched people who are very uncomfortable on the mountain top. We have brought many of them together on Sunday mornings in a non-threatening, informal, dialogue-driven atmosphere. Some of them have expressed their disbelief; others have voiced their doubts. In the valley, they have experienced severe pain, and most of them are wounded. The last thing they need is condemnation, disapproval, and rejection. Some of them have come one time and never returned, but most of them keep coming back, because they are looking for acceptance, not approval . . . for help, not a handout. We've watched many of them come to the mountain top where God has forgiven them. We've then watched them go back down into the valley to lead others to the top of the mountain.

It may be uncomfortable for us to be in the valley. It's risky, and we'll get our hands dirty. Suppose divorced people and alcoholics start coming to our worship services? Dirt, guilt, problems, shame, and embarrassment are in the valley. But that's also the very reason God wants you and me to be there. People in the valley desperately need to hear the message of grace and forgiveness that we can share.

Once in a bandshell at Daytona Beach I attended a rally of more than ten thousand students. The next day was Sunday, and at worship an unbelievable scene unfolded that I'll never forget. On the first row of that church was a middle-aged woman beautifully dressed, wearing a hat. Two guys—one with a Michigan T-shirt, and the other with a University of Notre Dame T-shirt—came and sat down beside her. Both had long hair and neither looked like the typical church goer. She scooted all the way to the end of the bench so she wouldn't have to sit near them. She didn't want to be in the valley.

Several years ago a young man in California, who normally didn't attend worship, was on his way to worship with his family. His father was a songleader for the church. Just before they got to the church building, the family saw a car wreck. The family wanted to stop and assist, but the father said he couldn't stop because it would make him late for the worship service. They didn't stop, and a lasting negative impression was made on his son—he vowed he would never go to that kind of a church again . . . and he hasn't.

When you're in the valley, you'll surely meet people with whom you disagree and people who are dirty. Some of them don't look like you either. They're of different races, subcultures, and religions. Some of them have no religion at all. Are you ready for the people with problems to come and sit by you? Are you ready to share their pain? Are you ready to help shoulder their burdens?

Jesus never ran from the valley. The Gospels don't record that Jesus ever ran anywhere. He had one foot on earth and one foot in heaven. For Him every moment was eternal and sacred. He knew who He was, and the angels encouraged Him to hold on because He was coming home, and they were going to welcome Him. They bring the same message to us as Christians.

That's what worship is all about—to remind you of who Jesus is and who you are. You are His beloved child. Know that. Believe that. Be so secure in that truth that you can leave the top of the mountain and go down in the valley to minister to hopeless people. There will be lots of opportunities for you to serve. The rich people in your city are in the valley and have the same problems as the poor. They have learned that money can buy some things, but it can't buy relief, hope, joy, and meaning.

Are you ready to go into the valley to serve with Jesus? Are you committed to the ministry of Jesus and reconciling people—all people—to God? Like Jesus, you don't need to run either! Rather, you need to keep your promise to follow Him faithfully, even through the valleys.

Thinking It Through

Opening Your Heart

The title for this chapter is "Jesus Never Ran."

• Does this title fit the commitment which Jesus made to worship and ministry? If so, how? If not, why not?

Digging Into God's Word

Read Luke 6:12-17. Explore the priorities which Jesus practiced for worship, community, and ministry.

• Why can't ministry precede worship and community?
• Why is solitude like first base in baseball?
• What happens when we place community last?

Taking It Home

It's unlikely that you and your friends are all on the same base at the same time.

• Which base do you think you're on right now?
• How do you think you can move to the next base in your life?

Chapter 9
For Better, For Worse

My uncle, Bill Staggs, comes from a humble and modest home in Portland, Tennessee, where he was his parents' only son. When World War II broke out fifty years ago, Bill went into the Air Force. He was trained in Texas, then went to Southern California where he flew night training missions. All of this was to train him to fly a P-51 Mustang. He was in combat almost daily in Europe and became the captain of a P-51 squadron with more than thirty planes under his supervision.

Very early one morning, before the sun rose over the English Channel, his squadron went out on a mission.

Only four planes returned. Uncle Bill went to war as a young man and returned an old one. Though he was highly decorated, his life, like thousands of others during that period of time, was totally disrupted.

When Uncle Bill returned to Tennessee, Mom and Dad invited him to come and live with us. He was a war hero, and he became one of my heroes too. We roomed together, and he became my best friend. He was looking for stability and calmness. Many times he would awaken in the night with horrifying combat experiences flooding his mind.

He began taking courses at Vanderbilt and later graduated from the University of Tennessee. That's where he met Betty, a girl from the Sequatchie Valley in East Tennessee. They married, graduated from college, and began their own life near Dunlap, Tennessee, where they reared five children. Eventually Betty suffered from Alzheimer's disease and required full-time care. Uncle Bill faithfully visited her several times each week. They were married almost fifty years by the time of her death.

Bill and Betty Staggs were among the 2.3 million couples who headed down the aisle at the end of the war. In the February 12, 1996, issue of *USA Today,* an intriguing story entitled "WWII Unbreakable Bonds" caught my attention. An amazing 16.4 people out of every thousand people in this country got married in one year: 1946. It's a record that stands today. These couples, who listened to Glenn Miller's music and bought a loaf of bread for ten cents, are celebrating fifty years of marriage. They watched the world change, but they stayed together. Dr. Terry Hargrove a family therapist of Amarillo, Texas, says, "They have a survivor mentality. They're a real stick-to-it generation, and that has carried over into their marriages."

In a book Gayle Prather co-authored entitled *I Will Never Leave You: How Couples Can Achieve The Power of Lasting Love,* she says, "By the time they reach the marrying age, they had already been through difficult times. That allowed them to survive the difficulties. In 1946 one out of every five marriages made it to fifty years. Today the average marriage lasts about 7.2 years."

Neil Howell, co-author of *Generations, the History of America's Future 1584 to 2069,* says, "I think their marriages staying together reflects the whole ethos of that whole society. Cooperation, teamwork, following through on the long-term promise. You did it, you built it, and the commitment was forever." Today, when commitment doesn't seem to be forever, listen to the words of Jesus from a time very much like today. A group of religious Jews came to Jesus and asked, "Is it lawful for a man to divorce his wife for any and every cause?" (Matthew 19:3). He replied,

> Haven't you read that at the beginning the Creator "made them male and female? For this reason a man will leave his father and mother and be united to his wife, and the two will become one flesh. So they are no longer two, but one. Therefore, what God has joined together, let man not separate."
>
> "Why then," they asked, "did Moses command that a man give his wife a certificate of divorce and send her away?" Jesus replied, "Moses permitted you to divorce your wives because your hearts were hard. But it was not this way from the beginning. I tell you then anyone who divorces his wife, except for marital unfaithfulness, and marries another woman commits adultery." (Matthew 19:4-9)

Christ restates the marriage plan as conceived by the Trinity. From the beginning, marriage is more than an arrangement or a contract involving two people. It's not like a business deal or a treaty between nations. Something more is going on.

Marriage is Forever

What is it that God knows about the importance of commitment between a man and a woman in marriage? Sometimes I sit in my office counseling a couple, who are talking about divorce, and one or both is extremely upset. I say to them that God does not have a divorce plan; He only has a marriage plan. In the very beginning it was God's plan that, if a man and woman wanted to live together, they should marry. That commitment is forever. Why? What's behind that? What is it that God knows about the marriage commitment that we need to know?

God knows that marriage is forever. In the beginning Jesus said that it was one man, one woman, and their God who made them one flesh. That doesn't sound like very good math: 1+1+1=1. The sexual relationship, as it is described beautifully through the Word of God, is a metaphor for the deep oneness that is in marriage. That oneness has to do with loyalty, companionship, and understanding. It has to do with the total giving of yourself to another person. But here's the clincher: Oneness is achieved by God and represented in marriage.

The late minister, Batsell Barrett Baxter, in a sermon entitled "The Greatest Human Contract," said, "Marriage is an agreement by which a man and a woman consent to live together as husband and wife, mutually accepting all of the responsibilities that this relationship entails and properly expecting all of the privileges and rights. The certificate of marriage is issued by the state, but the promises made are binding in the sight of God."

As I sometimes say in a wedding ceremony, the promises that you are about to make are not simply a civil contract involving a man and a woman and the state, but a spiritual relationship between the two of you and your God. One man plus one woman plus one God equals one flesh. And as Richard Dobbins said, "The closer a man and his wife get to Christ, the clearer they see how important it is for them to stay close to each other."

"The family," write David Stoop and James Masteller in *Forgiving Our Parents, Forgiving Ourselves*, "is meant to be an intersection of two covenants: a horizontal covenant between husband and wife, and a vertical covenant between parent and child." Promises, covenants, and vows are the foundation for marriage.

Two things in our society undermine God's plan of marriage being forever.

A lack of careful and prayerful consideration in preparing for marriage. We like the Cinderella story, or some variation of it, where boy meets girl, boy and girl look at one another, and it's love at first sight. Rockets go off, and they feel good about one another, so they marry. However, there's a major problem with that romantic notion: Love never happens at first sight. That's the error in the storyline. If you're thinking about marriage, prayerfully and carefully select the person you want to marry. Stay away from impulses based on flimsy feelings, and go for the heart. Decide in your will. You're making a lifelong commitment of trust to that person. Ask Bill and Betty Staggs.

As one unnamed writer said, "What's so remarkable about love at first sight? It's when people have been looking at each other for years that love becomes remarkable!"

A second problem that undermines God's plan for marriage is *a lack of genuine understanding of marriage.* To complete the story of Cinderella: Boy meets girl, love at first sight, rockets go off, they get married, it's in the stars—they live happily ever after. But here's another fly in the ointment. Bill and Betty Staggs would tell you that even though they were both Christians and reared five children who are now having children, it wasn't exactly a happily-ever-after life. They shared some tough times, too.

There was the time one of their sons, named Jim, was working at a summer job and was on a roof doing some work. He slipped and fell, hit his head, and was in serious condition. Another time, a car accident took another person's life. But they weathered the storms *together*. They stuck to each other and lived up to their forever commitment, as God intended.

Marriage is not "happily ever after." Every single morning she does *not* look exactly as she did the day they married, and in all fairness, he does *not* look exactly as he did the day they married either. That lack of genuine understanding, that kind of Hollywood idea that "if I'm married I will be happy all the time," is immature and leads to marital disaster. Your personal happiness is not the goal of marriage. The Cinderella thinking that *I'll feel great toward him or her all the time, and if I don't, I must not love him any more* is simply a misunderstanding of what real marriage is all about.

Gary Smalley in *Love Is a Decision* put it this way: "Every enduring marriage involves an unconditional commitment to an imperfect person." And Cecil Osborne went on to explain in *The Art of Understanding Your Mate* that "There are no perfect marriages for the simple reason that there are no perfect people, and no one person can satisfy all of another's needs."

Ann Malone, a good friend, told me about her mom. A doctor was interviewing Ann's mother for a video clip that he would be sharing with Texas medical students on how to care for a family member in the home. The doctor asked her mother if she ever got tired of caring for her husband. "Yes, my arms get tired when I stand by his bed to feed him, and my back gets tired, but I don't get tired on the inside." Marriage is forever, but it cannot survive in an on-again, off-again, he-loves-me, he-loves-me-not mentality.

There is something else God wants us to know from the teaching of Jesus in Matthew 19. God knows that there are unbelievable benefits to a life commitment. Here are three:

A life commitment offers the greatest opportunity for a couple to understand each other. You really don't get to know your spouse very well in the first two or three years. You may not even get to know them in the first seven years. One of the unfortunate things about divorce today is that marriages are ending before the husband and wife have an opportunity to get to know one another. A marriage goes through certain passages, just as a person does, but divorce ends the marvelous opportunity of experiencing the various passages of marriage. We mistakenly think that our marriage partners will respond and behave the same way we do if they love us. What we don't count on are the vast differences between men and women and the different ways they come at marriage in the name of love.

I didn't know how my wife Barbara would respond to certain kinds of pressures and stresses until the 1972 Southern California earthquake hit only a few miles from our house. I watched her take a broom and dust pan and sweep up the broken china and crystal, many of our wedding gifts. Then I listened to her pray to God and thank Him that we were alive and that our three children were not hurt. Then I knew how she would respond to a crisis.

You don't know how someone is going to respond to children until you rear children with them. You don't really know how someone will react when the heat is on and times are difficult until it happens. When the curfew has been broken, and you plan to discipline that child, will your spouse back you in that discipline?

Faith questions will come from your children: "Mom and Dad, why do we go to church? Why do we believe the Bible is from God? Why do we baptize? Why do we eat the Lord's Supper? Why did you become a preacher?" When those tough faith questions come, then you'll know what your spouse is really made of and what he or she really believes.

Now, as we deal with aging parents, I'm knowing Barbara better still, and because we have lived in Missouri, Illinois, Southern California, Seattle, and Dallas, I know her better. Marriage is a dynamic relationship. Our relationship is never static or the same from day to day. When you make a life commitment, it offers you the best opportunity and enough time to understand that other person.

A life commitment forces a couple to face life's realities. Love in a marriage means many things, including sharing, caring, giving, helping, listening, protecting, and touching. But love also means something else. When you are committed for life and conflicts come, you don't run from them. When there are problems in a marriage, you don't sweep them under the rug but you meet the real issues of life face to face. Love means that you will cope with lots of adversities as a team, a partnership.

It may be the issue of a child. You hope your new baby will be normal, but maybe your newborn has special needs. It may be the issue of where you plan to send your child to school. Who's going to spend six or seven hours a day forming the mind of your child? The question may be where you plan to live. What church will you attend? It may be whether your child plans to go to college or not. A life commitment based on shared promises forces a couple to face genuine reality. It causes you to deal with yourself and your spouse as you change. And we do change.

The time came when my dad told me, "Your mother is a great woman, but she is now becoming very weak." I couldn't imagine her being weak, but he knew her best. They were married over sixty years. Life changes, and so we change, and with that change must come adjustment, flexibility, and coping.

I appreciate what Ruth Senter said: "When true love comes, that which is counterfeit will be recognized. For someday it will rain on the picnic, ants will sting, mosquitoes will bite, and you will get indigestion from the potato salad. There will be no stars in your eyes, no sunsets on your horizon. Love will be in black and white with no piped-in music. But you will say 'forever,' because love is a choice you have made."

Adversity makes us stronger. The stronger the winds, the mightier the oak tree. Pressure can make us stronger, too, as the unknown poet has written:

> Looking back it seems to me,
> All the grief that had to be
> Left me when the pain was o'er
> Stronger than I was before.

Ask any couple who has been married more than fifty years, and they'll tell you that when they walked through the valleys of adversity, they were able to get to the mountain peaks of tranquility. Certainly the most difficult valley for any married couple is to bury one of their own children. You really wonder how a couple will ever make it after that. In fact, more than 70 percent of marriages break up after the death of a one of their children. But I have known several couples who have gone to the cemetery to bury a child and then walked together for years in commitment to each other in a very successful marriage. Commitment and keeping the promises they made are the keys.

A life commitment in marriage reinforces our growth and maturity. Married love is not simply based on feelings but on something more permanent. Recall the words of Paul:

> Submit to one another out of reverence for Christ. Wives, submit to your husbands as to the Lord. For the husband is the head of the wife as Christ is the head of the church, his body, of which he is the Savior. Now as the church submits to Christ, so also wives should submit to their husbands in everything. Husbands,

love your wives, just as Christ loved the church and gave himself up for her to make her holy, cleansing her by the washing with water through the word, and to present her to himself as a radiant church, without stain or wrinkle or any other blemish, but holy and blameless. In this same way, husbands ought to love their wives as their own bodies. He who loves his wife loves himself. After all, no one ever hated his own body, but he feeds and cares for it, just as Christ does the church—for we are members of his body. (Ephesians 5:21-30)

Married love is based on the recognition that we will grow and mature. Underneath that change the constancy of trust holds it together. Suppose we get married at twenty-two or twenty-three years of age. We're both working, and we trust each other. Then the children come along with school, travels, and all kinds of childhood struggles. We run car pools to little league games and ballet recitals. Meanwhile, trust is the glue that holds the marriage together.

Then the children become teenagers, and they choose a college and a career. Trust still binds us together.

There are trips and temptations everywhere, but trust helps us avoid them and holds us together. Then comes retirement and the latter years—"the last for which the first was made," as Robert Burns once described them—but trust still holds our relationship together "until death parts us." Without trust, marriage disintegrates at the first blow.

I fell in love with the Garretsons in Missouri several years ago. When I think about trust, commitment, and loyalty, I remember a letter my friend Walter Garretson wrote to me:

> As you know, for the past four-and-a-half years my wife has been stricken with an infirmity which has grown from (her being) a partial invalid to total invalid. For the past two years she has needed what I consider total care in every area of activity, both day and night. I knew my patience was wearing thin, and I fought desperately against that. Hundreds of times, if not thousands, I have prayed fervently to God to give me greater patience. But I could see no change, and I wondered why.

Then one night, after I had been up several times caring for her, in desperation and total frustration I threw up my hands and almost shouted to God: Father! Oh my Father! You know my plight! You have promised in so many places in your Word to answer your children's prayers! You know how many hundreds of times I have asked you to answer my prayers for more patience! Why don't you answer me? What have I done? What do you want me to do? And then I hung my head in remorse and asked God's forgiveness for my impertinence and weakness of faith.

A few days later I found myself taking my wife to Fremont Manor Nursing Home. I noticed how patient and kind the girls were who cared for her. After three-and-a-half months, though I visited her every day, I became so utterly lonely without her, I brought her home again. She has been home now for six months, and her care has intensified to such an extent that I even have to spoon feed her and turn her over in bed. She is completely helpless.

But the point I want to impress upon you is that now my patience is a thousand percent, or even more, better than it ever was before. I can see so clearly now that God was answering my prayers all along and is continuing to do so, not in the way I asked, but in his own way and in his own time. Not only that, but he has taught me a lesson I shall never forget. God answers prayers of faith according to his will, and he sometimes makes us participants in the answer to our own prayers.

Now, even in the middle of the night, before entering her room, never knowing exactly what to expect, I do not ask God to hand me the answer to my prayer on a silver platter. I ask him to give me strength to cope with what must be done. And he answers me. Praise God!

Fidelity

There is something else that God knows about a life commitment to marriage that is critical. The strength of a marriage commitment hinges on *fidelity*. The New Testament talks about it, but there's an Old Testament

Promises to Keep

book that beautifully displays it—Solomon's Song of Songs.

This book has clearly caused difficulty for rabbis and preachers. It's the account, dialogue, and poetic communication between Solomon and his wife. They are talking about their love, commitment, love-making, and their marriage. I called a rabbi one day and asked him how he was taught in his rabbinical training to interpret Song of Songs.

He said, "Well, they taught us that Solomon represents God, and his wife represents Israel."

I chuckled and said, "That's interesting. Conservative scholars have interpreted this to mean that God is represented by Solomon and that the church is represented by his wife."

Then I said to him, "Suppose it does not *represent* either? Suppose it's simply the beautiful thing that it purports to be? Where in the Bible does it ever say Solomon represents this or his wife represents that? Suppose, instead, we should assume the literal interpretation of Scripture of a husband and wife showing and talking about the immense fidelity of their marriage relationship?"

For example, Solomon's wife says, "All night long on my bed I looked for the one my heart loves; I looked for him but did not find him. I will get up now and go

196

about the city, through its streets and squares; I will search for the one my heart loves. So I looked for him but did not find him" (Song of Songs 3:1, 2).

As you continue to read, you begin to understand why she didn't find him. He was on a business trip representing Israel. It's the same thing that happens today when one of you goes on a business trip. You're separated from your spouse, and fidelity keeps you faithful to that person, because even though they are out of sight, they are *not* out of mind.

"How beautiful you are, my darling! Oh, how beautiful! Your eyes behind your veil are doves. Your hair is like a flock of goats descending from Mount Gilead" (Song of Songs 4:1). Now guys, if you go home tonight and tell your wife that her hair is like a flock of goats descending from Mount Gilead, be sure she understands that what you mean is that her hair is beautifully curly. Or, if you say to her, "Your teeth are like a flock of sheep just shorn, coming up from the washing. Each has its twin" (4:2), be sure she understands that you mean you think she has beautiful teeth.

Solomon also said to his wife, "Your lips are like a scarlet ribbon; your mouth is lovely" (4:3). "Your neck is like the tower of David, built with elegance" (4:4). Solomon's wife must have been beautiful.

"Your two breasts are like two fawns, like twin fawns of a gazelle that browse among the lilies. Until the day breaks and the shadows flee, I will go to the mountain of myrrh and to the hill of incense. All beautiful you are, my darling; there is no flaw in you" (4:5-7). There is no leering, no obscenity in these statements, but the beautiful and secret communication between the husband and wife as they talk together and share their love. Underneath it all is fidelity and commitment.

"Place me like a seal over your heart, like a seal on your arm." In other words, let everybody know that we are married. Men who are married should wear their wedding rings and talk about their wives in front of other women, letting everyone know that they are married. "For love is as strong as death, its jealousy unyielding as the grave. It burns like blazing fire, like a mighty flame. Many waters cannot quench love; rivers cannot wash it away. If one were to give all the wealth of his house for love, it would be utterly scorned" (8:6, 7).

Watch a Christian couple who have been married fifty or sixty years. They will hold hands and silently communicate to each other. Or they will steal looks at one another that are charged with love and understanding. Love is like a blazing fire. It is as strong as death, and it is permanent because the fidelity is unbreakable.

A few years ago I taught Song of Songs at a state university and asked the students to write down ten characteristics of this marriage. Not a person in the room, to my knowledge, was a Christian. These are the traits those university students identified:

1. Respectful
2. Open
3. Beautiful
4. Honest
5. Patient
6. Giving
7. Trustful
8. Romantic
9. Emotional
10. Sincere

Fidelity is what undergirds commitment. We ask couples to make this vow just prior to pronouncing them husband and wife: ". . . in sickness and in health, for richer, for poorer, for better, for worse, and keeping myself for you only, till death do us part."

Seventy-five percent of Americans today strongly agree that faithfulness is essential to a strong marriage, according to Andrew Greely in his book *Faithful Attraction*. Eighty-four percent of wives and 75 percent of husbands say that being married for life to one person is crucial, because the essence of the marriage commitment is fidelity. The intimacy and vulnerability of marriage requires ultimate trust . . . nothing less.

In an article entitled *How Do You Build Intimacy in an Age of Divorce?* Caryl S. Avery said, "Today trust is in short supply . . . Faith is no longer fashionable . . . with one of two new marriages ending in divorce and countless others existing in name only, trusting someone to be honest and committed over the long haul is increasingly difficult."

On a fall afternoon in 1997, I was parking my car at a retreat center in Colorado Springs, Colorado, when I recognized Bill McCartney, the popular football coach. McCartney took the University of Colorado to a national championship, but in the process, McCartney almost lost his own wife through neglect, and he left coaching in order to save his own family. (You can read his story in detail in his book *Sold Out* [Word Publishing, 1997].)

McCartney was coming to the retreat center as the founder of the new Promise Keepers men's movement. We stopped and talked for about thirty minutes and shared some of our experiences at universities, in marriage, and in family. One of the seven promises that

McCartney exhorts men to make is Promise #3 . . . *"to practice spiritual, moral, ethical, and sexual purity."* Coach McCartney is quick to point out that 62 percent of men attending Promise Keepers meetings struggle with sexual sin in their lives. No other issue comes close. Regardless, of how you may feel about the Promise Keepers movement, it clearly calls men to faithfully keep their promises made in marriage and in family. Men need to be encouraged to be faithful in marriage in today's highly sexually charged atmosphere.

I often hear single people say that it's hard to find someone to trust for life. What is it that breaks that trust? Jesus says it's marital unfaithfulness (Matthew 19:3-9). It begins in the heart and ends in a broken commitment. There are danger signals that come first. Movies depict fatal attractions and dangerous liaisons. Afternoon television makes adultery appear routine and even glamorous. Cheap papers sell scandalous stories of infidelity and distrust. One such writer says, "Trash sells; trust doesn't."

Betrayal, whether real or perceived, undermines fidelity, and thus commitment, in marriage. It's what my wife calls "emotional adultery." It never starts in bed. It starts in the elevator, at the water fountain, over a cup of coffee, at the copy machine, or in chat rooms or on the internet. A third of all romances begin in the workplace. *"Between 6 and 8 million Americans enter into a romance with a fellow employee each year,"* reports *U.S. News & World Report* (December 14, 1998). It seems to start innocently, and before long there has been an emotional break in the trust and commitment of a relationship. Today's cubicle is tomorrow's bedroom.

What is marital unfaithfulness? Some would say it's sexual union with anyone other than your spouse, but this is not a complete reading of the Bible. Marital unfaithfulness in the Old and New Testaments is literally a sexual term but it is often used figuratively as a covenant term. God indicted Israel for *breaking covenant* with Him or for marital unfaithfulness (Jeremiah 3:8, 9; Isaiah 57:3). He painted Israel as a covenant-breaker, a promise-breaker, an adulteress, who was unfaithful to Him as the marriage husband (Hosea 2:1; 4:11-15; 5:7; 9:1).

In the New Testament, James called faithless Christians "adulterous people" (4:4) because they had broken their covenant with God. The Bible teaches that we can break covenant with God in many ways (Matthew 12:39; 16:4; Mark 8:38; 2 Peter 2:14; Romans 2:22; Revelation 18:3, 9). The essence of marital unfaithfulness is infidelity. From the beginning God has had a marriage plan focused on fidelity. Jesus had but one divorce/remarriage plan (Matthew 19:8). All other reasons for divorce and remarriage are concessions to His original dream. Fidelity is the key. A couple must replenish their trust in each other on a daily basis, because their marriage is at stake.

Three Suggestions

Here are three proven ways to increase trust and show that you intend to keep your marital promises:

Never threaten your spouse with divorce. I knew a wonderful couple who had been married sixty-eight years. On the day of their anniversary, as we were celebrating with them, I asked if she had ever threatened divorce. She looked at me with a smile on her face and replied, "No. Murder many times, but never divorce!" They never talked about divorce as a possibility.

When I contacted Harold and Roxie Thomas and asked them to write a special article about being married sixty years for *21st Century Christian* magazine, they wrote that they never ever discussed divorce. It was not an option; so they never threatened it. Couples like Harold and Roxie don't even joke about getting a divorce, because it's truly not funny.

Show your commitment to your spouse. I will never forget getting on a plane in Missouri and recognizing a pulpit minister from a large denominational church.

He was seated several rows ahead of me. On our flight, he took off his wedding ring and began to flirt with one of the flight attendants. It was so disappointing to see this middle-aged preacher trying to "come on" to a young, confused lady.

Protect your marriage. Do everything within your power to strengthen it. Never create doubt or confusion about your commitment to your spouse. Marriage is not a joke. It's a life commitment that needs protection, a serious promise that must be kept, and you are the only one who can do it.

Keep your promises to your spouse. You make your commitment for life when you marry, but you build trust and fidelity by daily keeping those initial promises. Remember that our culture will not help you keep that promise and will give you no support or encouragement to be faithful. Rather it will picture infidelity as the norm and unfaithfulness as the rule. Regardless, God calls you to be faithful to Him, and to measure this, He watches to see if you keep your promises to your spouse.

I first met Joe and Sarah in Southern California in the late 1960s. Their story is fascinating and true. During the dust-bowl days, they left Oklahoma for Long Beach with absolutely nothing but each other. Their only hope was to move to Southern California with some of their friends so they could make a living. Joe worked with his hands, and he worked extremely hard. They raised a family together, and they never let the pressures of the depression or World War II move them away from their commitment to each other

During their long marriage, Joe collected lots of stories. I used to visit them in a nursing home in Granada Hills, California, and our visit would make my day. Joe would start one of his long, funny stories and I would look forward to the punchline. But Sarah had heard all of his stories many, many times. She knew all of the punchlines; so she would begin to laugh long before he would end his story. It was wonderful to see her laugh, even though she knew all of his stories.

I was saddened to get a phone call one day telling me of Joe's death. "Would I perform his funeral service?" "I would be honored," I said. Shortly after Joe's funeral, Sarah returned to the loneliness of her room in the nursing home. Joe had always been there before. Their marriage of over sixty years had not brought much money, but it had brought them together in a deep sense of oneness. One night, just before going to sleep, Sarah called in one of the nursing attendants and gave her some final instructions. With Joe no longer there, she turned over in her bed, went to sleep, and died in her sleep. All of the nursing attendants believed that

Sarah did not want to go on living if she had to face life without Joe. After all, many years earlier in Oklahoma she had made him a promise: "for better or for worse." Marital commitment is forever.

Thinking It Through

Opening Your Heart

Some marriages have been described as "the bind that ties" instead of "the tie that binds."

- What are some of the "binds" of a marriage?
- Describe an experience or make a suggestion about something useful, helpful, or life-changing in dealing with any possible "binds" of a marriage.
- What outlooks or approaches have freed-up your relationship to God and to your spouse?

Digging into God's Word

In Ephesians 5:21-32 Paul compares the relationship of Christ with His church to a marriage.

- How can you put verse 21 into practice?
- What have you learned about the value of submission? Why is it so difficult for a marriage partner to be the first to submit?
- How does Jesus submitting to the cross help us learn how to submit to each other?

Taking It Home

Hopefully, you have learned some practical lessons on commitment to your marriage.

- Have you observed this kind of commitment in close friends that are married?
- Pray daily for your marriage for the next month.
- Make some specific promises to God about how you will practice greater commitment in your marriage.

Chapter 10

Saving Your Child's Life

I remember it as if it were yesterday. It was actually March of 1965, and Lori Ann, our first child, had just been born in Southern California. Alberta, Barbara's mom, had come for Lori Ann's birth, and we were so glad to have her. She helped bathe and dress Lori Ann; she changed her diapers, rocked her to sleep, and supported Barbara and me in every way she could. She also assisted with cooking and cleaning.

Then, two weeks after Lori Ann's birth, Alberta said, "Prentice, tomorrow would you please take me to the airport so I may fly home to Nashville?"

With a shocked expression I blurted out, "You can't go home yet. Why, who's going to take care of Lori Ann?"

"You all are," she said.

That was one of the first moments when I realized the tremendous responsibility of being a parent. The next day, I drove Alberta to the airport, kissed her good-bye, and drove back home to Culver City. That night Barbara and I took turns checking on Lori Ann to be sure she was breathing. Barbara was more comfortable than I was with this new role. I thought, *With my luck, I'll mess up, and Lori Ann will have a problem.* Well, she not only made it, but today she and her husband, Scott, are having their children. Barbara and I feel a certain thrill watching our children raise their own children.

Sometime later, while serving on the Missouri Committee for Youth and Children, we selected this poem by Mamie Gene Cole entitled "The Child's Appeal" from the book *Religious Masterpieces* to be the frontispiece for our fact book:

I am the Child.
All the world waits for my coming.
All the earth watches with interest to see what I
    shall become.

Civilization hangs in the balance,
For what I am, the world of tomorrow will be.

I am the Child.
I have come into your world, about which I know
  nothing.
Why I came I know not;
How I came I know not.
I am curious; I am interested.

I am the Child.
You hold in your hand my destiny.
You determine, largely, whether I shall succeed or
  fail.
Give me, I pray you, those things that make for
  happiness.
Train me, I beg you, that I may be a blessing to the
  world.

While in college I helped finance my education by working as a lifeguard and swimming instructor. It was fun to watch people get in the water. Some were comfortable in the water; others were not. On a few occasions I had to rescue a person from dangerous water. In a similar way, we will have to save our children's lives from threatening waters. Consider the dangerous waters swirling around our children. They face fear of the future; peer pressure; uncertainty; failure; and competition.

We adults sometimes think the word "danger" is an adult word. But when children in Hanover, Massachusetts, sign up for stress management seminars, when suicide becomes the number-two killer of our youth, and when record numbers of teens drop out of school, the word "danger" also applies to our children. Many of our children who turn to drugs, run away from home, and drop out of school have serious problems with their own self-image.

While living in Los Angeles in the 1960s, I spent some time talking to young people on the Sunset Strip in Hollywood. By the way, the average age on the Strip was thirteen. One Friday night I talked with a 13-year-old girl from Philadelphia.

"I bet you miss your parents and they miss you," I said.

"Are you kidding?" she laughed. "My dad uses our home as a filling station. He comes home on weekends, gets some clean clothes, repacks his luggage, and leaves on Monday. He doesn't care about me or where I am."

I never saw her again, but I've thought about her several times. Like so many of our children, she felt no sense of worth or value, especially to her family. Her story leads me to suggest the ways we parents can save our children's lives.

Help Your Child Grow Taller

I vividly remember a football game played in the midwest. There were no bands, no half-time performances, and no cheerleaders. The game was not significant because of ratings, but it was very important to one little boy. The game featured little boys called "Mighty Mites" ages 7-8. When a pile-up occurred during the game, it just looked like a huge stack of football equipment, because you couldn't really see the tiny boys.

On one play the offense carried the ball to the right, blocked the end, and ran for about ten yards. On the next play, they did it again for about twenty yards. On the third play, they ran the exact same play for a touchdown. Each time the defensive end was blocked for a big gain. Then the most unbelievable scene took place. The father of the boy being blocked ran onto the field, lifted his son up in the air, and then threw him in the dirt and shouted angrily, "A son of mine will make the tackle!" That night, a little boy went to sleep wondering if he was a good boy. After all, we can't always "make the tackles."

There is a basic principle from antiquity that has no exceptions: "As a man thinks in his heart, so is he" (Proverbs 23:7). It all begins in our earliest moments as children. As far as God is concerned, the business of liking yourself is the most basic of all. Parents may spend tons of money on braces, piano lessons, computers, and sports for their children, but if it doesn't contribute to self-worth, what real value is it?

Since self-worth is so crucial to our children's success, consider these suggestions:

Affirm the accomplishments of your child. Don't tell your child, "You're such a good person." As your child gets older, he or she won't believe you. But if you praise his achievements, however small, he'll believe you and feel self-worth. "Good catch." "Sing that song again." "That dress looks so nice on you."

Touch your child, and he'll know he has value. In a major survey of families in Southern California, the University of Southern California found a father's touch to be most important to building a child's self-worth. Hug, hold, touch, and your child will feel valuable.

Expect the best of your children. When you do, they'll do their best. But if you call them "stupid," "idiot," "ignorant," or "dummy," they'll give you their worst. Remember, children live up to the names you call them. Catch your children doing something right and tell them.

Motivate, Don't Manipulate

H. L. Menken, famous feature writer and reporter for the *Baltimore Sun*, once stood on his desk in the news room and shouted, "It's overwhelming us. It's covering our desks and soon will cover us."

"What?" someone replied.

"Mediocrity," Menken replied. With that, he left the newspaper and never returned.

Boredom, apathy, and mediocrity confront our children on every hand. They have nothing to do and too much to do it with. They know that most Americans don't vote. They come to understand that Good Samaritan Laws are passed to require action and responsibility in crises. They hear adults say, "I don't want to get involved." As Soren Kierkegaard once said, "This age will not die from sin, but from lack of passion."

More than ever, we parents need to hear the wise words, "Train up a child in the way he should go and when he is old he will not turn from it." (Proverbs 22:6). I've known of parents who've manipulated their children and used this verse as a proof-text, but that is to misunderstand Solomon. The phrase "in the way he should go" may be literally translated "according to his own way." God has built into every child "his own way"—a way to reach his heart and soul. If you have more than one child, you know how different your children can be from each other. One may be quiet, introspective, and feelings-oriented. The other one may be loud, aggressive, and intellectual. You're to motivate each child in accordance with what is most appropriate for him or her. Find the unique path that leads to each of your children's hearts.

So how may we motivate our children to rise above mediocrity, do their best, and achieve their goals? Consider these practical suggestions:

Find your child's natural bent. I once asked my mother how it was that her parents raised two successful children. She laughed and said, "Here was my dad's philosophy of child rearing: Find out what your child wants to do, and help him to do it!" If you think about that for a moment, there is a lot of wisdom in it. Find your child's natural, God-given bent and help him develop it. If you were to do a family profile and sketch out the temperament, abilities, capabilities, and characteristics of each of your children, you would not only see how different they are from one another, it would help you to find each child's natural tendencies.

Expose your children to people you admire. Children need heroes. Child experts tell us that the very first heroes of children are their parents. We must seem like giant-sized people to our children. Sometimes they play games and act like us, wear our clothes, and try to walk in our footprints. But as children grow older and parents become less idealized, our children turn to others for heroes. Think of people you know who are of solid character and high achievement and, if at all possible, have them in your home so your children can know them, too.

Model high achievement in your own life. Some parents are non-achievers, while others make things happen in life, even reaching beyond the normal limits. Parents who work hard tend to have children who are highly motivated. I've always thought it was important for my children to understand my work. Perhaps you could take one of your children to work. When they see you model in your own life accomplishment, achievement, and work, you are helping to motivate them to reach their goals.

Guide Your Children By Keeping Up Your Fences

While living in Southern California, Barbara and I came home from the grocery one day to find a young teenager sitting on our door step. As a little boy, he had been taught to steal from supermarkets by his dad. He had the horrible experience of seeing his father later kill himself with a gun. A compassionate Christian family had adopted him, but he had been in trouble with the public schools, the police, and other young people. He was about to run away from home, but we persuaded him to go back to his parents who loved him and cared for him. His life was out of control with no boundaries, no fences, and no discipline.

As an immediate solution, he went into the military. Early one morning he cursed his drill instructor, who struck him in the mouth with his weapon. The blow broke his jaw in four places. While the drill instructor may have acted beyond the military code, the broken jaw certainly woke this young man up. At the end of his training, I received a letter from his Commander-in-Chief which informed me that this young man was receiving the highest award for his unit. He had finally learned discipline and responsibility, but that's a tough way to learn it. Children need boundaries, fences, and limits. Here are some suggestions on how you can guide and discipline your own children.

Communicate that you have a reason for building fences. The goal of parental discipline is self-discipline. When your children see that you have a solid reason, that you know right from wrong, that you have solid ground on which to stand, they will begin to develop ground on which they alone can stand. No wonder the Bible frequently urges moms and dads to guide and lovingly discipline their children.

Define the limits of your child's behavior. Set limits on the kind of language they can use, time limits (e.g. curfew), the use of the car, responsibilities for certain jobs at home, decisions they can make, money they can spend, and expectations of the family. Parents who are fearful of setting limits will cause their children to pay a very dear price in the future, but courageous parents, who set limits for their children, have the foresight to train their children for a society that has limits as well.

Practice fairness and allow for exceptions. Successful families have rules, but they also practice fairness. Barbara and I have learned that it takes a lot of wisdom and a lot of humility to practice fairness. But if you'll treat your children as God treats you, you will not only have rules, but flexibility. Both are important.

For a number of years I had three sermons on how to raise children. Then Barbara and I had three children, and I can still picture the garbage can where I threw those three speeches. What you learn in rearing children is not learned in any other way. Hopefully, your experience will draw you closer to God and closer to them.

I particularly like the words of Hodding Carter who has written, "You can give your children two lasting gifts—one is roots, the other is wings." Within your hands are the tools to help your own children become a blessing to the world. Let's not disappoint them!

Thinking It Through

Opening Your Heart

Three main suggestions are given in this chapter to save your child's life. Pick a favorite and explain your reason for your choice.

- Help your child grow taller.
- Motivate; don't manipulate.
- Guide your children by keeping up your fences.

Digging Into God's Word

Many times Jesus lifts up a child as a model for Christian living today. Turn to Matthew 19:13-15, and read this example.

- How are the kingdom of heaven and a child similar?
- What is there about a child that is so precious and God-like?

Taking It Home

Children in today's world are in deep trouble. Even in the best of homes, greater attention and love need to be devoted to our children.

- Which of the suggestions in this chapter best fits the needs of your family?
- How might you begin to implement these suggestions?
- What specific prayer needs do you have as a parent?

Chapter 11
Honor Your Father and Mother

I clearly remember the last time I jumped on one of our children for turning over a glass of milk at the supper table. In the process of correcting her, I turned over my own glass of tea. Sometimes all you can do is just laugh! It's really the best thing to do because so many things that happen in our families are really funny.

Why is it we cry our hardest and laugh our loudest about our families? Certainly no group is as intimate, as close, or as ancient as the family.

The Bible is really the story of families. First, Adam and Eve, then Noah and his family, then Abraham and Sarah, Isaac and Jacob, and the stories of families continue in the great Word of God. The entire nation of Israel comes from a single family. And when Jesus came from heaven to earth, He became a part of a specific family.

With all of those families there are problems and difficulties, as well as highlights and joys. The Bible tells of both. But today's family seems to be in deep trouble. The very respected British paper *The Economist* has recently said that in America families are valued tremendously, so much so that most people have at least two of them. There's no doubt that our families today are in jeopardy. Commitment to each other seems to be crumbling.

If there was ever a time we need to turn back to the Ten Commandments, it is now. Few people have any moral code today. And the Commandments sound strikingly relevant to us. The first four Commandments are vertical—about your relationship to God. Commandments five through ten are horizontal—about your relationships to other people. Let's look at just one.

The Fifth Commandment

God said, "Honor your father and mother so that you may live long upon the earth." Why does God say that? What is it He wants us to understand that He already knows? What does it really mean to *honor* your parents?

Don't we owe a huge debt to our own parents? How will you ever repay your mother for giving birth to you? How will you ever repay your dad for putting food on the table for you? How will you ever repay your parents for the time they invested in you, for the moments of love they gave you? Have you ever done something so embarrassing and discouraging that you really wondered if you could face the future? Yet, you knew your parents were the people you could always go back to, and that they would receive you. Robert Frost, the American poet, wrote, "Home is the place where, when you have to go there, they have to take you in."

Unfortunately, I'm sure you know some parents who are not good examples to their children. Drug and alcohol addictions, physical and other forms of abuse, desertion, divorce, unconcern, and even suicide by parents leave deep emotional, and sometimes physical, scars on their children that will never go away. Yet, honoring your parents in spite of their worthiness or worthlessness, in spite of the tragedies of your own life, is the most healthy, Christlike, mature way a person can respond. Is it difficult to do sometimes? Oh, yes! But it *is* possible with the help and strength of the Lord.

In 1900 one out of four Americans lived beyond age sixty-five. Today, three out of four live beyond sixty-five. By the year 2040, about 21 percent of Americans will be over sixty-five. To have our parents and grandparents living much longer is a special joy to many families.

Barbara and I are part of the first generation of Americans who will probably spend as many years taking care of our parents as we spent taking care of our children. We have found this responsibility to involve many questions and difficult decisions. Charles Swindoll has written, "Growing old, like paying taxes, is a fact we all must face." But I'm not going to say when growing *up* stops and growing *old* begins—no way!

My Story

In November 1996 my cousin Steve, who is a physician, visited with my 80-year-old parents and found my dad extremely short of breath. Dad was admitted to the hospital where tests showed congestive heart failure. The doctor scheduled surgery to remove fluid around his heart and provide a window for any future fluid to drain away from his lungs. I flew home and my sister Linda and I visited with Mom and Dad about death and dying issues. Thankfully, it was a comfortable subject for the four of us to discuss. I mentioned to them that Linda and I had no legal power of attorney, no way in which to make medical decisions in case one of them became unable to make their own decisions. While the attorney had Mom and Dad sign powers of attorney, Dad looked up and said, "Why in the world did we wait until now to do this?"

After successful surgery, Dad's doctor told him that he and Mom needed to sell the family house and move into a safer care setting where they could have some supervision. The doctor was trained in family medicine, had excellent communication abilities, and took lots of time with Mom and Dad. Mom and Dad represent a generation who listen to authority figures, so they listened to him when he instructed Dad to take a driver's test.

Some time after Dad left the hospital, he scheduled his driver's test. This was not the state driver's test, but a one-hour test of eyesight, reaction time, and driving on both freeways and city streets. To my knowledge he had never had a driving test like this one. Instead of the test being administered by a uniformed police officer who was an authority figure, it was given by a young lady. Wrong! And when she told Dad he had failed the test, he said some harsh things to her and went home angry.

On my next trip home, I took Dad out for a drive and told him, "I love you very much. You're my dad. You must call or write this young lady (who had given him the test), apologize to her, and ask for her forgiveness." He did and was so successful in talking with her that he talked her into giving him another driver's test. They again drove the streets and freeways for an hour. She passed him. Here we go again!

In February 1997 we had Mom and Dad's house ready to sell. On the first Sunday after the sign went up, forty-seven people came to see it. When I asked Dad how the day had gone, he only said, "We didn't sell it!" Clearly, he was disappointed. I tried to explain that most people don't sell their houses on the first day with several inches of snow on the ground. There is a time of offers and counter-offers, and, of course, over the next few weeks there was. But it really didn't matter how much money was being offered for their house, it would never be enough for them. You see they weren't selling a *house*, they were selling their *home*. They felt they were leaving *memories*, not *property*.

Finally, Mom dug her heels firmly into the ground. "I'm going to die in this house; I'm not leaving it alive." She said it with her fourth-grade-teacher voice—the voice of authority and finality, and there was no wavering. With a smile on my face and firmness in my voice, I told her that she had exactly twenty-nine days in which to die, because the house would be sold at that point. Mom and I have a great rapport, and we had just come to an impasse, but I knew that we had to carry out our plan. I think she knew it, too, down deep in her heart. Over the next twenty-nine days she cried her tears but was ready to leave when the house closed. (Whether I was prepared to become Mom's parent or not, that's what she needed in this situation.)

Members of our family converged on the old house for the last time. We packed on Saturday and separated things for the garage sale, the new apartment, and throw-aways. On Sunday we gathered in the old house for a final time and worshiped. Dad mentioned all the great memories they had of people who had been in their home over the previous thirty-eight years. There were preachers, missionaries, people from other nations, students, Christmas dinners, and Thanksgiving feasts. We laughed and cried as each of us told of a memory connected to the house. We sang and prayed and shared the Lord's Supper, because worshiping God seemed the most appropriate thing that we could do as we were about to leave the family house. After all, in the earlier years of that house, Linda and I had our faith strengthened, had many questions answered, and had made some very important spiritual decisions.

By Monday morning the furnace and the automatic garage door opener wouldn't work. As they left to close on the house, Dad cautioned Mom, "Please don't say a word about either the furnace or the garage door. Don't say a word." So they went to the lawyer's office and immediately Dad said, "Reckon we ought to tell them about the furnace and the garage door opener?" As soon as everybody stopped laughing, they closed on the house.

As we were moving furniture into a moving truck, Mom and Dad came for one last look at the house. Mom walked out of the house, down the steps, down the sidewalk, and to the driveway without a tear in her eyes. She had already cried her tears. She didn't want to leave, but she knew she had to go because it was the best thing for them. Dad walked from room to room, then down the front steps and out into the front yard. It was a yard he had mowed many times. He looked at the old house, shook his head, and thought of lots of memories. He and Mom had lived there for nearly forty years. Finally, like an old Southern gentleman, he tipped his hat to the old house as if to a grand old lady and walked to the car.

The family spent the next two days moving Mom and Dad's things into their new apartment at the care facility, unpacking, putting up pictures, and arranging everything for them before they arrived. It was important to them that they have their bed, their furniture, their pictures and their wall pieces. Linda and I had only three things in mind: to keep them together, to provide 24-hour medical emergency care, and to give them a high quality lifestyle. Whenever you move your parents out of the old family home and into a new care facility, you run the risk of being thought of as bossy, mean, distant, and unloving. Some people might even think that if you really loved your parents you wouldn't be moving them out of their home.

After Mom and Dad were in their new home, Linda and I turned from "bandits" into "heroes." We were greatly supported by special close friends, Mom and Dad's accountant, attorney, and physician, and we found that this team approach to caring for our parents was an indispensable component to the success of the move. We met as a team prior to the move in order to discuss every possible option for Mom and Dad. Even after Mom and Dad moved into their new home, we continued to function as a team, and I will always be grateful for each person's willingness to contribute.

Their apartment was wonderful. It was on the third floor overlooking a beautiful lake where ducks and geese lived. They had a large living room, a comfortable bedroom, contemporary kitchen, a small den, a well-furnished bath, and a covered patio complete with their own patio furniture. They selected the apartment and their own furniture to go in it. Fully carpeted, the apartment also had an excellent security system. It was such a great security system that when Dad was trying to get into the facility one night and couldn't, he used his friend's car phone to call Mom in the apartment. She immediately pushed the emergency button. Within seconds a security guard and nurse showed up at her door. She told them, "Dad is locked out and you all need to go and let him in." They promptly obeyed her as if they'd been in her fourth grade class years earlier. They also reminded her what the security button was really all about.

Mom and Dad made new friends in their new home. Mom is especially outgoing and friendly. She was meeting another lady for the first time and after the lady gave her name to Mom, my mom said, "Now you'll have to tell me your name again when I see you because I may not remember it." The lady chuckled and said,

"Why honey, if we had good memory, we wouldn't be living in a care facility." Mom laughed.

Of course, none of this happened without constant communication. Linda and I tried to listen carefully to Mom and Dad. We asked for their advice, and we tried to express our concerns in ways that would emphasize our respect and love for them. We brought their own professional advisors into the discussion circle. On any number of occasions Linda and I expressed our personal concerns to Mom and Dad. We respected their decisions and tried to listen carefully to them with regard to their medical condition and their desires for the future. In turn, they leaned on us, listened to us, and accepted our advice and counsel. Communication is absolutely a key when dealing with your parents as is patience.

In late May of 1998 I was invited to give public lectures on Christianity in the Cultural Palace built by Josef Stalin in Rostov-on-Don in southern Russia. Even though Dad was quite ill, he blessed my trip and wanted me to present those lectures. On Sunday afternoon, May 31, I came to the conclusion of the final lecture on the theme of "Security in Christ." For some reason, even though it was not in my notes, I decided to illustrate security by telling them the story of my dad's faith, his illness, and his assurance in Christ for all eternity. I noted to the audience, "Dad is extremely ill back in the United States. He and I talked about the fact that we may not see each other again here upon the earth, but we will be together throughout all eternity. That's because of security in Christ Jesus."

Life is filled with paradoxes! What I didn't know as I gave the final speech was that back in the United States Dad was dying in the arms of my mother. She later told me that as she held his head, he just slipped away as though he left the room. The nurse standing by Mother said, "Mrs. Meador, you can let go of him now; he's gone away." I didn't know of his death until I returned to the United States.

Our family gathered to plan how we would remember Dad. Families can choose between tragedy or celebration, and we chose celebration. A huge crowd in Nashville joined us as we gathered at the Hillsboro church building and sang, prayed, cried, and laughed. Friends, fellow elders, and family members recalled his dedication to Jesus Christ, his great service and Christianity, his hard work, his learning to laugh at life, his humility, his lack of fear, his love of family, and his display of wisdom. In 1926 G.C. Brewer baptized Dad in Portland, Tennessee. S.P. Pittman married Mother and Dad in Springfield, Tennessee. Dad was a Christian for seventy-two years and was married to

Mom for sixty-one years, served as an elder of the Hillsboro Church of Christ for thirty-five years, taught the professional and business women's Bible class for forty-one years, and worked for the United States Postal Service for thirty-eight years. In a time of change, transition, and mobility, something is to be said for longevity and commitment. A man with a great sense of humor, in his last conversation with his brother-in-law, Bill Staggs, Dad said, "Bill, many a fish is alive and well today because we are weak and old." We celebrated his great service in Christianity, including short-term mission work in Australia, England, and several American cities. A strong supporter of Christian education, he was called David Lipscomb University's "Number One Fan" by the Nashville *Tennessean*. Appropriately, a memorial fund was established in his name at David Lipscomb University to assist students who want a Christian education.

Of course, we are so pleased that we had already moved Mom and Dad into their new apartment where they had made new friends and adjusted to independent living. I'm certainly not an expert on the subject of "Parenting Your Parents." I'm not even sure that experience is always the best teacher. I've had lots of experiences where I've missed the main lesson, but I'm sharing some experiences with you that I've learned in the care of Mom and Dad. I've done so in order that it might prepare you for some different lessons that you'll be learning as you care for your parents. I've shared the story of caring for my parents because they have meant so much to my life, and I thank God every day for them. I have respected them, cared for them, and I'll continue to provide for Mom. I'll always be grateful to them.

By the way, sometimes actions speak louder than words.

Thinking It Through

<u>*Opening Your Heart*</u>

This chapter begins with a funny story about a parent turning over his tea while correcting his child for turning over her milk at the supper table.

- Why do some of the highest joys and deepest pains occur in family?
- Describe a humorous event that happened in your family.

<u>*Digging into God's Word*</u>

In Matthew 15:1-11 Jesus revealed how God expects children to care for their parents. He revealed how the Pharisees tried to find a loophole around this commandment.

- Read this passage for yourself. What standard of care are we expected by God to give our parents?
- Are Christians expected to care for their parents this way today? Explain your answer.

- Examine what Jesus did for His own mother while He was on the cross (John 19:25-27). Is Jesus our model for caring for our parents today?

Taking It Home

This chapter calls for more involvement and commitment on the part of children to care for their parents when parents can't help themselves.

- How does this chapter provide you with a plan for caring for your parents? Or does it?
- What are some current needs your parents are facing, and how can you assist? What problems/hurdles does this present for you?
- Make some plans of how you will care for your parents, and pray about your plans.

Chapter 12
Throwing Away Our Scorecards

Bruce Larson and Keith Miller, in their book entitled *The Edge of Adventure,* wrote: "The neighborhood bar is possibly the best counterfeit that there is to the fellowship Christ wants in His church. It's an imitation dispensing liquor instead of grace, escape rather than reality, but it is a permissive, accepting, and inclusive fellowship. It is unshockable. It is democratic. You tell people secrets, and they don't tell others or even want to. The bar flourishes not because most people are alcoholics, but because God has put into the human heart the desire to know and to be known, to love and to be loved. So, many seek a counterfeit of a few beers."

With all of my heart I believe that Christ wants His church to be a *fellowship* where people can come in and say, "I'm sunk; I've had it. I'm taking off my mask. I'm hurting, confused, in need of a friend."

- Where do you turn when the bottom falls out of your life?
- To whom do you go?
- Do you have anyone to go to?

It's clear in the movie *Contact* that Jodie Foster, who played an astronomer, was saying, "I don't understand with all the science and technology that there is in the world, why is there so much loneliness." What science may have promised is friendship. It may have promised to overcome the loneliness and alienation that we all feel at times when we are looking for someone to whom we can turn. We want a shelter, a refuge, a listener. We need someone who understands. David had Jonathan, Ruth had Naomi, and Paul had Barnabas.

⌐A Model of Friendship⌐

The great model of friendship is our Lord. There are several basic things Jesus did that model for us how to be a friend. They are the colors in the portrait of friendship, the threads woven into the tapestry of friendship, the piano keys that produce harmony in the music of friendship. Each is valuable on its own, but together they transform our relationships with each other.

Alienation and depression are epidemic. Many people are looking for friends. Samuel Taylor Coleridge said, "Friendship is a sheltering tree." Do you have the branches of friendship under which to shelter yourself? Sadly, most people don't seem to have anyone to listen to them, to affirm them, to love them. Their tree is bare, the branches stripped of sheltering foliage.

Jesus spent time with His friends. Toward the end of His life, Jesus had already spent almost every waking moment for three years with Peter, Matthew, John, Andrew, and the rest of the apostles. "Jesus called to him those he wanted . . . that they might be with him" (Mark 3:13, 14). He chose these men in order to be able to spend time with them (Mark 9:30, 31). At times Jesus didn't want anyone to know where they were because He was teaching His disciples. He would pull the twelve apostles away from the multitude and spend time just with them. "Come with me, by yourselves to a quiet place and get some rest" (Mark 6:31). He spent nearly every moment of three years of ministry with these twelve men. In that time they got to know Him, watch Him, and learn from Him.

Friendship takes time—lots of time: time to laugh, to cry, to fuss, to repent, to care, to touch. Time to trust and time to disclose. So Jesus didn't choose a thousand men, but twelve. He could devote himself in three years to only twelve men. He could build a relationship with each one—Philip, Bartholomew, Peter, James, and the other eight. In three years Jesus could show His trust, express His appreciation, resolve His conflicts, and disclose His nature to twelve men. Jesus understood something our age of microwave potatoes, one-minute cereal, and instant happiness doesn't quite get—friendship takes time.

There's something else Jesus did in the time He had with the twelve apostles. He knew the value of feeling valued. The pages of the New Testament give a lot of press to Peter, James, and John. From the transfiguration to the Garden of Gethsamane, these three are given plenty of attention. What about James the son of Alphaeus or Thaddeus? You begin to wonder if they're really players on the team! Stars like Peter or John knew they were important, for they heard it from many people, but James and Thaddeus had crucial roles to play as well. And Jesus affirms, praises, and instructs them to be His friend, share their faith, and take His cause to the world. They were needed and He let them know it.

Jesus allowed us to look at friendship from an interesting vantage point—from the standpoint of His friends. "That which was from the beginning which we have heard, which we have seen with our eyes, which we have looked at and our hands have touched. This we proclaim concerning the word of life" (1 John 1:2). Jesus lived. We saw Him, testified to Him, and we proclaim to you the eternal life which was with the Father and has appeared to us. We share with you what we have seen and heard so that you also may have fellowship with us. We had fellowship (friendship) with Him. In that three years of Him spending time with us, we looked at Him, saw Him with our eyes. The life appeared and we stared at Him . . . gazed at Him. We watched to see if He would turn the other cheek when He told us to. Jesus allowed His friends to see Him, to measure Him for consistency, to view how He dealt with people. John tells us what happened out of that friendship. It was so revealing that Jesus showed God, the Father, in the time they spent together.

Jesus committed himself to His friends. "No one has greater love than the one who lays down his life for his friends" (John 15:13). Jesus carefully and prayerfully chose these men as His friends. "This is how we know what love is. Jesus Christ laid down his life for us. We ought to lay down our lives for our brothers" (1 John

3:16). That's what friendship is—being committed to your friends, willing to lay your life down for them.

——————————
——————————

The sports world took note of the special friendship between Gayle Sayers and Brian Piccolo of the Chicago Bears football team. In an era of racial hatred, these two men may have been the first bi-racial roommates on an NFL team. Sayers and Piccolo took a lot of flack for their friendship. Blacks were supposed to room with blacks, whites with whites, so their friendship broke ground in race relations. Even their spouses became close friends.

When Sayers hurt his knee, Coach George Halas assigned Piccolo to Sayers' position as running back. Sayers went into rehab but began to slack off after a few sessions. So Piccolo urged him to work harder to regain his former position. "I don't want to take your position; I want to earn it." Sayers, due to Piccolo's constant encouragement, regained his position in the backfield.

When Brian got cancer, Gayle was there for him with reinforcement, encouragement, and hope. Even though Brian later died from his disease, Gayle Sayers continued to talk about their friendship, their closeness, their trust, their time together, and their commitment to each other.

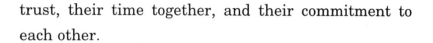

Jesus' relationship with His friends contrasted greatly with the Pharisees who were members of the royal order of religion and who were constantly judgmental, hating one another. They were the back-stabbers of religion. So Jesus says, "I want you to love one another and commit to one another as I am committed to you." This is one of the threads in the tapestry of Christian friendship.

Jesus communicated with His friends. "I no longer call you servants because a servant does not know his master" (John 15:15). Some employees have no idea what management is doing. Contrast that with what Jesus said: "I no longer call you servants because a servant doesn't know his master's business. Instead I call you friends. For everything I learned from my Father I made known to you." I didn't keep anything back; everything God told me I passed on to you. He told me how to share with you what the kingdom of God is about, and I shared that with you in the parables. He has told you through me how to get along with your mother and dad, with your spouse and children, and I have shared that with you. I have even told you how to get along with the authorities. You are in on the Father's business. You and I have the deepest level of communication possible, because that's what you have with friends—you take the mask off and put your feet up on the hassock. "Friendship is a sheltering tree," where you are refreshed and renewed.

Jesus knew that the key to relationships is communication. In His conversations with his apostles, He was transparent. No secrets. No hidden agenda. Nothing to hide. He showed them His tears, His fears, His anger, and His plans. And Jesus valued each one as a special person. Aren't you impressed that He treated them as equals, as peers? He was heaven at home on the street, the Creator eating bread with the created, holiness holding hands with the less than pure, yet Jesus met people where they were and accepted them for who they were, and His acceptance empowered his friends. Peter, a fisherman, was empowered to fish for people. James and John, sons of thunder, wrote about love, compassion, and service to others.

Jesus' encouragement gave the apostles a dream of something greater than themselves. "The knowledge of the secrets of the Kingdom of God have been given to you, but to the others I speak in parables" (Luke 8:10).

They didn't fully grasp what He meant, but He didn't give up on them. He continued to accept them though they didn't have a clue. Only after He was gone did they see that their mission was to change the hearts of people, not to chase the Romans out of town. He conveyed His confidence in them. Jesus believed in and communicated with His friends.

Jesus had conflict with His friends. Jesus said, "Are you all so dull?" (Mark 7:18). Are you ever going to get the point? Don't you love the story of the thousands of people in upper Galilee around the Horns of Hatten where they came to hear Jesus? Jesus had five loaves and two fishes. More importantly, He was the Creator of all fish and bread—the Creator of everything. He hoped His friends would figure out that all He had to do was say the word and He could feed them all. Instead, standing by the omnipotent Creator, they looked around and said, "Where in the world are we going to get enough food to feed all these people?" I once heard a Rabbi say, "You know Jesus could have made enough bagels for the entire dessert." But His friends had missed the point again; so Jesus said, "Are you all so dull? Are you ever going to understand?"

Jesus didn't give up on them though; instead He took them down to the lake and walked on the water. He patiently and repeatedly showed them His power. But they turned right around and did it again, Mark said. They still had not figured out that He truly must be the Son of God. And He said to them, "Do you still not see or understand? Are your hearts so hard?" (Mark 8:17). "Peter, get behind me. You are full of Satan" (Mark 8:32-33). Jesus had huge conflicts with His friends.

I don't have any conflict with the lady at the grocery story who bags my groceries, but then I don't know her, and she doesn't know me. We don't know each other's names, we don't spend any time together, and we don't converse. We rarely have major conflicts with people we don't know. Conflict normally comes when we have relationships with others. We argue with our spouses, children, parents, and friends. Why? Because they are close to us, and we care about them. Conflict can be an index of how close we are to others. Jesus had conflict with His friends because He cared about them. If He hadn't cared about Peter, He wouldn't have said a word to him. If He hadn't cared about the apostles, He would have just chosen a new group of followers.

Jesus forgave His friends. In some ways, this is the secret to Jesus' relationships with Matthew, Peter, John, and the rest. "If your brother sins against you, go and show him his fault, just between the two of you. If he listens to you, you have won your brother over" (Matthew 18:15). Of course, Jesus never asks us to do something He has not already done. How many times does Jesus go individually to one of His friends, build a bridge, heal a wound, and leave in peace? Jesus knows we don't handle conflict well; we're not prepared for it, we misunderstand it, and we take conflict very personally.

Perhaps, we've used the wrong model. So many of our churches have patterned themselves after the business model driven by achievement, profit, and efficiency. Royce Money in *Building Stronger Families* points out the paradox of such a model: "The institutional church finds itself in an ironic situation. On the one hand, the church stands for and promotes good family relationships. On the other hand, it may be fostering the opposite in its practical effects. If we believe that the church is more like a family than anything else, that one concept will have profound effect on the modern business model some of our churches have unwisely adopted."

In business, when a mistake is made, someone pays. It's the punitive cycle approach. As a colleague once said to me, "Prentice, the word 'forgiveness' is not in either the business nor the academic vocabulary."

There we keep scorecards on each other, and mistakes deserve punishment. "Turn the other cheek" is for women and children but not for the real world. It's a dog-eat-dog world, not a dog-forgive-dog world!

As Sigmund Freud said, "One must forgive one's enemies, but not before they have been hanged." Wall Street, sports, business—here they react just as I did when Dudley hit me on the playground in the second grade. I hit him back. It just feels natural to hit back, keep score, punish. In a competitive, all-or-nothing world, we love to win, to be on top. Forgiveness seems like losing. But Jesus calls you to throw away your scorecard on others. Why? Because He threw yours away:

- "Forgive them Father . . . ."
- ". . . he who is faithful and just will forgive our sins and cleanse us from all unrighteousness."
- " . . . in whom we have redemption, the forgiveness of sins."

Why must you throw away your scorecard? Because He wants you to imitate Him, to be like Him: "Be kind and compassionate to one another, forgiving each other, just as in Christ God forgave you."

I don't think we create forgiveness. It's more like floating in the current of God's forgiveness, like allowing His forgiveness to flow around and through us. When we refuse to forgive, we're fighting against the current of Divine forgiveness. So John warns us "Do not be like Cain" who hurt his brother. But be like Christ who "laid down his life for us" (1 John 3:12-16).

But how do we learn to throw away our scorecards? I think we learn to forgive from those who've already learned forgiveness. Clearly, the master forgiver is Christ. Others have followed His example. After suffering in one of Hitler's death camps, Martin Niemoller said, "It took me a long time to see that God is not the enemy of his enemies."

I'll never forget an evening in Dallas where Barbara and I had dinner with a survivor of Auschwitz. She told us of the fear, suffering, and pain she felt every day for years. The Nazis starved her, and she became so emaciated that she passed as a man. Now in her eighties, she described how she had forgiven those who tried to kill her. Where would you and I be if our parents and family kept a scorecard on us? I've noticed that forgiven people are the most forgiving.

Forgiveness of our friends and enemies is not optional—Jesus commands it. It isn't something outside the target; it is the bullseye of what relationships are really all about. I'm talking about "love." Love means that you stay committed to your friends. When they're in trouble, when they're sick, when they have offended you, love means that you are there for them. Jesus' dream is of a group of people who will act in a forgiving way toward each other, because He knows something we don't know—it's not only good for us, but it's the way people on the outside know we're the church. They see the tapestry and know it is woven with threads of love and forgiveness.

But do you notice something else Jesus models to us about friendship? Behavioral scientists, after years of research, tell us that the maximum number of friends is twelve. That's exactly the number of friends Jesus had. Then He had three very close friends—Peter, James, and John. They were His inner circle of friends, and we see them with Jesus in some of the most thrilling and difficult moments of His ministry. Then Jesus had one intimate friend, His best friend—John. While dying on the cross, Jesus gave the care of His own mother into the hands of John. You only do that if a friendship is intimate.

Several years ago, I had lunch with a professor of psychiatry at the UCLA Faculty Center. During our meal, we talked about friendship. He was a much older professor and had done a lot of research and reading on human relationships. I'll never forget what he told me: "Prentice, a person is very lucky to get out of life with one good friend! Most people never have one good friend." I thought he'd overstated his case, but now, I think he was right. Intimacy takes time, trust, investment, and deep love. You just can't have that with everyone. Most of us walk around in the shallow water most of the time, because we can only go into the deep water occasionally with one good friend.

The Stages of Friendship

There are three stages of friendship. First, you have a casual acquaintance with someone else. It's pretty superficial with casual greetings and responses that don't go beyond a quick exchange of words: "How are you?" "I'm fine. How are you?"

Stage two is relationship. Out of all these acquaintances you start talking with people, sharing meals together, spending time together, praying together. You start to know people on a somewhat deeper level. This is hospital time, funeral home time, wedding time, sharing time. Friendship.

The third stage is commitment. This is where you say to someone, "You are my friend, and I will never leave you." It's interesting the kind of conversation you can have with people like that. You can be away from them for a long time, but when you see them again, you just pick up where you left off as if no time at all has passed. You are committed to them, and they to you.

True friendship is a two-way relationship where you are refreshed, but where your friend is refreshed as well. It's a place of both listening and being heard. Isn't it interesting that in education we teach people to speak, to write, to add and subtract, to operate computers, but we don't teach them the art of listening? We assume we know how to listen, but often we are thinking of how we plan to respond while the other person is still talking. When that happens, we aren't listening. Or when we make a judgment about the other person or what the other person just said, we aren't listening. Genuine friendship is built on empathic listening. That's when I try to walk in your shoes, feel what you're feeling, understand what you're saying. And when I let you know that I feel or understand what you are saying to me, you feel a special worth, significance, value, and affirmation. That's how you know I am really your friend. That kind of listening is difficult, demanding, and exhausting but, oh, so needed for solid relationships.

I am so moved by the story of Roy Benavidez and his solid commitment to his friends. As told in The New York Times (December 4, 1998), Roy was born the son of a sharecropper in South Texas. Not long after birth he was orphaned and went to live with his uncle. Because he was needed to pick sugar beets and cotton, Roy dropped out of middle school. By the age of 19, he joined the Army and was sent on his first tour to Vietnam. He stepped on a land mine and doctors feared that he would never walk again, but he recovered. He was retrained and became a Green Beret and was sent to Vietnam on his second tour of duty.

On the morning of May 2, 1968, Roy heard a cry for help over his radio while at his base in Loc Ninh, South Vietnam. A twelve-man Special Forces unit had been ambushed by North Vietnamese troops in the jungle. Roy jumped into a helicopter and he and the pilot flew into a horrible fire fight. As he leapt off the helicopter, Roy was shot in the face, head, and right leg. But he continued to run toward his friends in trouble. He found four dead and others wounded. He dragged the survivors aboard the helicopter but then enemy fire killed the pilot and burned the helicopter. Roy got the troops off the helicopter and for the next six hours returned fire, administered morphine to the wounded, called in air strikes, and recovered secret documents. He was shot again and again in the stomach, thigh, and back. A North Vietnamese soldier bayoneted him, but Roy was able to kill him with a knife.

When Roy was taken back to Loc Ninh, he was unable to speak or move. All assumed that he was dead and his body was being placed in a body bag. Suddenly he spit into the doctor's face to signal that he was still alive and was evacuated for surgery in Saigon. On February 24, 1981, President Reagan presented the Medal of Honor to Mr. Benavidez at the Pentagon. He lived with two pieces of shrapnel in his heart, a punctured lung, and was in constant pain from his wounds. World famous for his devotion to his fellow troops, Roy Benavidez lived until the age of 63 in San Antonio. He once said, *"I don't like to be called a hero. I just did what I was trained to do."*

"No one has greater love," says Jesus, "that the one who lays down his life for his friends. You are my friends if you do what I command" (John 15:13, 14). No wonder the church in its best moments is a network of friends, modeled after Jesus and His own personal relationships. It's so important for us to move from casual acquaintances in the church to committed relationships. By spending time with two or three people, you can begin to slowly take off your own mask. Start with some small things. I think John Powell is right when he said, "Why don't I tell you who I am? Because I'm afraid if I do you will reject me." So a lot of us live in our own self-imposed prisons, surrounded by loneliness. Let's begin to take our masks off. Your best chance of being accepted is with people who have already been accepted by God. If you want others to throw away their scorecards on you, go to those for whom God has already thrown away their scorecards.

Friendship is ordained and blessed by God. Based on shared promises, friendship is one of life's most crucial and rewarding commitments, and it is worth the effort.

Thinking It Through

Opening Your Heart

The chapter title, "Throwing Away Our Scorecards" involves forgiveness—not holding grudges, resentment, or bitterness.

- Why do we find it so difficult sometimes to forgive our closest friends and family?
- What do you think happens to us when we do not forgive?

Digging Into God's Word

In Matthew 18:18-35 Jesus tells Peter a story to teach him why reconciliation between Christians is so essential.

- Read this passage for yourself. Why do you think the man who was forgiven the impossible debt found it impossible to forgive a smaller debt?
- When Christians find it impossible to forgive, what does Jesus say happens?
- What is Jesus trying to teach Peter?

Taking It Home

Forgiveness is the lubrication that keeps friendship and family working.

- In a world that throws away cans, minutes, and people, what steps would you suggest to make our Christian friendships more durable?
- What experiences have you had where reconciliation made a friendship lasting?
- What "take homes" can you find in this experience of reconciliation that might make a difference for you in the future?

Chapter 13
The Guns Are Silent

The guns are silent . . . at least for today. The mountain behind me is dangerous ground. Yellow tape identifies the area of the mountain where thousands of land mines have been planted. This isn't the first time this mountain and coastline have been treacherous ground. Hatred has a long history here—at least back to the ninth century A.D. Tribes once fought here with swords and spears, but today men fight with mortars, tanks, and aircraft. Bosnia is nearby, because I am writing this from Croatia!

Yet, it looks so peaceful, deceptively so. I'm looking out at the Adriatic Sea with Italy not far away. It's a steel-gray day; rain glistens on the evergreens along the coast and its steady cadence makes me sleepy. The sea is unusually calm and rocks forming the sea floor are easily visible.

It may have looked this way about two thousand years ago when Paul came to this same coast and preached about Jesus. Then it was known as Illyricum (or Dalmatia). Paul specifically mentioned this region to the Romans (Romans 15:19), and he even seemed to be stressing his own commitment to preaching by pointing out Illyricum as a central place of importance or a point of extremity in the Roman world. Clearly, it was of key importance in Paul's ministry. In fact, Paul's own commitment to Christ led him to this very region because no one else had ever brought the message of Christianity here (Romans 15:20). Commitment meant planting the seed of Christ for the first time in open, receptive hearts in Illyricum. It is also important in the Christian movement today, and commitment to Christ, especially in the form of Christian service, still rings throughout this region. Doubtless, Paul would be proud.

To really appreciate such practical Christian service, though, first we must feel something of the *pain*. How do I describe what I'm seeing?

- Wounded, maimed people of all ages
- Dislocated persons who have lost everything
- Ethnic cleansing designed to eliminate an entire race
- Permanent damage to cities, villages, families
- Life on the edge

Pain so fresh, so horrible, so indifferent, so complete, so permanent. Pain so deep, there are no words to describe it, only tears. War is a strange, abnormal way of life that changes everything, marks everybody, and respects no one. It waits for nobody, regardless of who they are. What had seemed important no longer is—schedules disappear, routines are interrupted. War changes the reference points of daily life. It gives you a new set of eyes through which to see life with new perspectives, new needs, and new opportunities.

Even though the guns are silent, Croatia is a place of uncertainty. During the recent war with the Serbs, air raid sirens gave the people of Zagreb about two minutes warning. What happened in only two minutes? Trains, buses, taxis, and cars abruptly stopped and emptied. Stores cleared, and streets were quickly deserted. As people sought safety underground, the city stood still awaiting possible attack.

Attack came from Serbian planes, missiles, and mortars. A streetcar, not quite emptied in the center of downtown Zagreb, took a hit. Death and destruction came with surgical precision to government, military, and political installations. In the normally quiet villages surrounding Zagreb, families scurried to their homemade bomb shelters packed with food, water, and packaged foods. Due to one of the marvels of modern technology, some of the families cocooned in the shelters could talk on cell phones. Jets strafed the area. They suddenly appeared, seemed to hang in the sky above their targets, and quickly disappeared leaving behind explosions, destruction, and death.

After a war, like the one in Croatia, does its worst, God does His best. In fact, He does some of His very best work on a war-torn battlefield, in a destroyed village, or in a broken life.

Commitment Serves People

A few days ago, I met Emira and Dzemal just outside a small village on the Adriatic Coast which is not really their home. He was a postal worker, and she was a teacher of thirty-two years in the Bosnian town of

Prijedor. When the recent war came to their town, the Serb army attacked and occupied their house. For over three hours, the army held Dzemal at knife point threatening to cut off his head in front of their son. He knew they would kill him and his entire family. They taunted him until he was exhausted, but finally, they grew tired of terrorizing Dzemal and left for a moment. Just then Emira came home and found her husband and son hiding in the house, fearful of the army's return at any time. They had to run for their lives, leaving behind their house, furnishings, savings, friends, jobs, and their Muslim way of life.

They were driven to Varazdin, the city north of Zagreb, where they began contacting various humanitarian organizations for help. One of the first groups to respond was a congregation of Christians. They brought Emira and Dzemal pasta, flour, sugar, oil, tomato sauce, canned fruit and vegetables, a fresh chicken, winter clothes, and shoes.

A month later, the church gave them more supplies, including thirty pounds of potatoes. I met them when they came to a retreat where I was teaching some very basic perspectives about Jesus—who He is, what He did for others, what He can do today when a life is open to His power and influence. Emira and Dzemal looked tired, serious. They had seen a lot of pain, torment, and terror. Though Muslim, they didn't miss a session; they studied the Bible, filled in the lessons, and asked several questions. As I left them, they thanked me for coming and teaching them about Jesus. Here's the point: they came to the retreat because they had been served by committed Christians—people who fed and clothed them, Christians serving Muslims.

During the retreat, a short, stocky Bosnian woman sat near the back of the group. She looked extremely tired, even discolored, worn out from her recent war experiences. During my presentations, she often cried but said nothing, for her pain was too deep to discuss. She was a Muslim and the target of what the Serbs call "ethnic cleansing."

Once she owned a lovely three-story house in Bosnia, but she lost it when the Serbian Army confiscated and occupied it. Then she lost everything else, and she nearly lost her life when a bomb exploded and wounded her with metal shrapnel. She still has metal fragments in her head from the explosion. Doctors fear an operation will kill her.

She moved nervously and was seldom still. Her dreams of a peaceful life had been replaced by anxiety and uncertainty. Having lost everything, she was finally rescued and taken to Croatia. There Christians fed, clothed, and nursed her back to health. They also gave her a Bible, taught her about Christ, and today she is a Christian living in Croatia. While I may never see her again, I shall never forget her openness, her kindness to me, and her appreciation. But the real reason that I got to meet her is because some Christians served her even though she was a Muslim.

Dragica and Zlata, sisters in their forties, lived in the village of Slunjska, Selnica, located just across the Kupa River from the city of Karlovac. Fed by melting snows in the mountains, the Kupa abounded with trout and other game fish. When the Serbian Army attacked the village, it destroyed thirty-four of the thirty-nine houses and occupied the other five houses for military purposes. Dragica was widowed when her daughter was seven years old. When the war broke out, Dragica's father, mother, and in-laws all lived with her and her daughter.

Having stayed in Slunjska, Selnica as long as they could, and fearing for their lives, they planned an escape. One night, they each took all they could carry, quietly pulling their new tractor with them. For three days they hid in the woods, walking at night and hiding during the day. They finally reached Karlovac, but it was too late for Dragica's mother, who died after reaching the town. Because the family was impoverished, they could not bury her in the local cemetery near the town, but they planned to move her body to the cemetery when they had the money. It seemed their lives would all end in tragedy, and they felt completely hopeless.

When Christians in Zagreb learned of their situation, they gave them food, clothing, and tools, including a wheelbarrow and garden equipment, to rebuild their lives. They also gave them a refrigerator, stove, and other appliances. Christians, whose compassion knew no boundaries in Croatia, served refugees.

Daruvar, a small city of approximately ten thousand people, is located about two hours drive east of Zagreb. In January 1992, just ten days after the cease fire, Mladen Jovanovic was invited to visit that war torn region. As a minister, Mladen had helped spearhead humanitarian efforts throughout Croatia. He was accompanied by Boris, an English language professor who was working for the Dean of the Medical School in Zagreb and who arranged for his trip.

"We traveled in Boris' auto to Daruvar. Then the mayor of Daruvar, the police, and Croatian army personnel took us to the cities of Pakrac and Lipik, just fifteen kilometers and twenty-two kilometers from Daruvar," said Mladen. "The destruction in these towns was unbelievable. We had difficulty finding a house with a roof. Of the few people still in Pakrac, eighty-seven were living in cellars. Approximately forty thousand people had fled the area to the relative safety of Zagreb."

"Daruvar had also suffered some destruction as the Serbs had fought their way to the center of the town and occupied the medical clinic for several weeks," Mladen continued. "There was really nothing of value left in the clinic. What they could not take with them was broken beyond repair or burned. Within a few weeks, we were able to gather some basic medical supplies for the clinic."

Mladen continued to describe Daruvar's overwhelming need: "The mayor, realizing our concern for the victims of the war, came to us with a special request. Forty-eight men, residents of Daruvar, had been killed during the fall of 1991 defending the city. The mayor asked if we could provide humanitarian help to the remaining families. For almost two years we made monthly trips to Daruvar and distributed food to these families."

One of the men who lost his life defending Daruvar was Katica's husband. Not really a soldier, he had worked for fourteen years in the local fish cannery near Daruvar. His death left Katica with a teenage son and two daughters, the youngest being seven. Katica "always notified the families when we were coming," said Mladen. "She invited us to her home many times for meals. In addition to massive amounts of food and clothing, we gave all these families Bibles and had many Bible studies with them. They felt so helpless and were without hope. We will only know when we get to heaven how many seeds took root and grew."

"Visnja came to us," according to Mladen, "with her young son of nine months to receive food the first month we distributed which was in March, 1992. The young boy was born two months after his father was killed. In spite of her grief, Visnja always came with a smile, a kind word of thanks, and many times she brought us small gifts of flowers or some cookies she had made."

On Christmas Day 1992, with the help of European Christians, a party was held for the children of Daruvar. "Slavko, a member of the Zagreb congregation, played Santa Claus. Other members of the Zagreb church presented some musical entertainment. One of the missionaries from France was with us and gave a Christmas message," said Mladen. "Over one hundred children, their parents, and other members of the community were present. The mayor arranged for us to use the auditorium of the local high school."

"We also gave gifts to the fifty-eight children living in the orphans' home at Karlovac," Mladen continued.

"which also included hygiene products and laundry supplies. Last winter, we were able to buy them a TV and a VCR. Our gifts of love have opened the door for greater things, too. Next year," said Mladen, "World Wide Youth Camps have been invited to teach the children Bible stories in their summer camp."

As I'm about ready to leave Croatia, I am struck by the overwhelming service of Christians to any and all people, regardless of race, creed, or religion. You may think I've been describing an army of volunteers numbering in the thousands. Actually, the number of servants is less than one hundred! Once again I'm awed by the paradox: The weaker the servant, the greater his strength. Remember that Paul quotes the Lord, saying, "My grace is sufficient for you, for power is perfected in weakness" (2 Corinthians 12:9)—just the opposite of our human way of thinking! Or again, the greater the adversity, the richer the service: "When I am weak, then I am strong" (2 Corinthians 12:10). All of this makes me wonder, *Who would have dreamed that God would use a war to reach Bosnian Muslims with the story of Jesus Christ?* Then I remember that early Christianity had its greatest growth during the Roman persecution. "The blood of the martyrs was the seed of the kingdom," wrote Eusebius.

Words are truly significant. Early Christians used a special vocabulary for several reasons:

- Words expressed their beliefs.
- Words gave them their identity.
- Words bonded them in unity.

Some of their words were "love," "atonement," "grace," "baptism," "redemption," and "faith."

Two of their most glorious phrases must have astounded the Romans—"slaves of Jesus Christ," and "keepers of the covenant." Now we know why. It's because they combined their words with their actions. They faithfully kept their covenant, their promises, and their commitment to Jesus Christ, just as slaves faithfully obey their masters. They kept their promises, even when it meant being abused and persecuted, even when it meant being ripped apart by lions in the Roman arena, even when they had to watch their mates murdered and their children tortured. Their words of promise and commitment were so much more than mere words—they were bonds of love on the heart, never to be broken.

Today, the guns are silent in Croatia, but the message from the Christians there rings loudly for us all. Your words of promise and commitment are not mere words to be tossed aside at the first obstacle either. To your friends, your family, your Lord and God, they are bonds of love and service on your heart, never to be broken. If you don't keep them, you're a coward; if you do keep them, you're a hero. Either you can live up to them, or spend the rest of your life living it down. It's really that simple, and it's your choice.

Thinking It Through

Opening Your Heart

This chapter stresses the power of pain and how it changes everything.

- Describe a time of pain in your life.
- How does war leave indelible marks on people?

Digging Into God's Word

In Matthew 25:31-46 Jesus describes the judgment day on the basis of responding to human needs.

- What is the real difference that Jesus sees between His people and those who do not belong to Him?
- What is the meaning of "compassion"? Is it just a feeling?
- Who is your neighbor?

Taking It Home

In order to make this chapter become a part of your daily life, think of some people who have genuine needs, both physical and emotional.

- What can you do to take care of some of these needs?
- How can you do it in the name of Christ without receiving any of the credit?
- Pray that God will continue to bring human needs and people with pain into your life.